A PRINCE OF THE CHURCH IN INDIA

Owing to the antiquity and rarity of this book, certain pages are regrettably absent, and readability is compromised due to the blurring of the original text. If you possess any insights regarding the availability of these missing sections, kindly inform us. Your assistance is crucial in ensuring the completion of this significant work for the benefit of future generations.

A PRINCE OF THE CHURCH IN INDIA

BEING A RECORD OF THE LIFE OF THE REV KALI CHARAN CHATTERJE

J. C. R EWING

GYAN

Published by

Gyan Publishing House
5, Ansari Road
Daryaganj, New Delhi-110002
Phone: 011-47034999, 9811692060
E-mail: books@gyanbooks.com

Distribution Network
gyanbooks.com
India, USA, Canada, UK, Australia

ISBN: 978-93-7014-518-4 (PB)

First Published, 1918

2nd Impression 2025

Printed at: Gyan Press, Delhi.

A PRINCE OF THE CHURCH IN INDIA
Arthur J. C. R EWING

A PRINCE OF THE CHURCH IN INDIA

A PRINCE OF THE CHURCH IN INDIA

, Being A Record Of The Life Of The Rev. Kali Charan Chatterjee, D.D., For Forty-Eight Years A Missionary At Hoshyarpur, Punjab, India

James Caruthers Rhea Ewing

Rev. Kali Charan Chatterjee, D.D. (Washington and Jefferson 1894, Edinburgh 1910). This portrait was taken in Edinburgh, Scotland, in 1910.

INTRODUCTION

NO one who ever saw Kali Charan Chatterjee during the last twenty years of his life will ever forget him. The venerable figure with the long flowing beard and the clear and tranquil eyes, the kindly dignified demeanor, the noble spirit abide in the memory. He was a character of no common quality, a personality of distinction. A long line of high Hindu ancestry lay back of him. As a boy he came under the kindling, transforming influence of the great missionary, Alexander Duff, and he passed out from that influence a changed man of firm and assured Christian faith and of unfailing Christian purpose. Those who declare that Christianity can not really reach the Indian mind or that no high caste Hindu can ever lay aside his Hindu conceptions and become a thorough Christian would have had their declaration utterly shattered in meeting Dr. Chatterjee. He was a Christian in spirit, in manner of life, in character, in conviction. He knew the Christian doctrine as well as any Western theologian. He lived the Christian life as truly as any Western saint.

Dr. Chatterjee was a thoroughly wholesome and well balanced character. He was not of the same type as that remarkable man, Nehemiah Goveh. Goveh was a saint of the sort produced by the imperfect commingling of a philosophic Indian personality with the sacerdotal and sacramental type of Christian. Dr. Chatterjee was deeply devout and he was a scholar of Indian philosophy and he was a lover of the Church, but he was a healthy, hearty active leader of men. He had good gifts of organization and managed a large mission station with all the efficiency of a Western administrator. In his work he won all men's friendship. The Indian people loved him and Englishmen and Americans held him in high esteem. For many years he ministered to the foreign community in his station as well as to his great flock of Indian Christians. He was the outstanding Indian Christian in Northern India. No leader of the Indian Church was more respected and trusted by Indians and missionaries alike. A few score men like him would change the whole religious situation in India.

Dr. Chatterjee was known both in America and Great Britain. His last visit was in 1910 at the time of the World Missionary Conference in Edinburgh where he was one of the conspicuous figures and where the University of Edinburgh honored itself and him together in the way described in the sketch. In all such associations, Dr. Chatterjee moved with ease and confidence and the perfect simplicity of his true and honest spirit.

No one in India was so well fitted to write this little memorial as Dr. Ewing. Dr. Ewing went to India in 1879 and no one else knew Dr. Chatterjee better than he. No one also knows the Panjab better. Dr. Ewing has spent all his missionary life there and would be selected by every one who knows the Panjab as the most distinguished citizen among all its European or American residents. He has served four times as Vice-Chancellor of the University of the Panjab, has been decorated and again and again honored by the British Government, and is held in unbounded confidence and regard by Mohammedan, Hindu and Sikh.

Dr. Ewing has condensed the story into the most compact limits. It is a noble picture which he has drawn of a rich and devoted life.

He has made no missionary argument, nor suggested any missionary apologetic. But no apologetic or argument could equal the appeal and evidence of such a life. The cause which can produce such men and hold their undying loyalty needs no other vindication or defense. One such man is worth any expenditure and from the life or one such flows influences which spread deep and wide through India and which abide forever.

ROBERT E. SPEER.

New York.

CONTENTS

ILLUSTRATIONS

I

BENGAL AND THE PANJAB

The ideals that lie at the heart of the Gospel of Christ are slowly but surely permeating every part of Hindu society and modifying every phase of Hindu thought.—*Sir Narayana Chandavarka.*

IN the history of Christian Missions in India, there have been few events of more significance than that which occurred in the City of Calcutta on a July morning in the year 1830. It was then that Alexander Duff opened a school, in which the English language was to be largely employed as the medium of instruction. It was his conviction that the time had come, when the learning of the West should be made available to the eager youth of the East, and that by making them familiar with the treasures of English Literature, he, as a Christian missionary, would be opening for them the way to an intelligent appreciation of the great fundamental facts of Christianity. This he believed would result in the dissemination of Christian truth amongst the multitude who would eventually be reached and influenced most effectually by their educated fellow-countrymen. The new method met with no little opposition. As an innovation, it startled many of those whose aims were identical with his own. Remonstrances poured in. It was predicted that the immediate result of the system would be to "deluge Calcutta with rogues and villains." That a brilliant scholar and orator such as he should devote several hours of each day to the task of teaching the English Alphabet to a group of Bengali youths, appeared to some the extreme of folly. To them it seemed nothing but hopeless and meaningless drudgery, and the devotion of one's time to it most reprehensible in a minister of the Gospel, who had been commissioned to "preach the Word."

As the years passed, the institution thus founded, became the center of a remarkable movement, affecting not only the growth of the Church, but less directly, the entire educational policy of the Government.

It is no part of the present purpose to deal with those great problems in Evangelization, concerning which widely divergent views have been held by good and wise men. It is enough to say here that the comparatively early outcome of the new method was such as to convince even the most sceptical and to lead to widespread imitation throughout the entire country.

His work opened a new missionary era in India. Western thought caused a great ferment in a multitude of minds. Shortly thereafter the English language became the official tongue of the Empire. That it should be so was decided at the Council Board of India under Lord Bentinck, and perhaps no more momentous decision was ever formulated there.

The results produced by English education in India are essentially revolutionary. To this new Education is largely due the awakening of the people, and the creation of a desire to have some share in the great world drama that is being played. Those who resolved upon this policy in 1854 were not incapable of anticipating the almost inevitable outcome of the scheme agreed upon. They were broad-minded enough to institute it and to await in calmness the result, seeing that in this way alone could the moral responsibility of England to India be discharged. All honor to the men who refused to share in a policy of keeping the people in comparative ignorance, although that would presumably have rendered the task of governing India less difficult and perplexing.

In the days of Alexander Duff the time was ripe for such an enterprise as his. There were practically no "half-way houses" between the more or less gross forms of idol worship on the one hand, and Christianity on the other. In the case of many who were no longer able to tolerate the grosser elements of their ancestral faith, the choice lay between an entire denial of all spiritual religion and an acceptance of, at least, some of the great truths which the Christian Scriptures had presented to their minds.

One after another, in spite of the most strenuous effort, failed to find any middle ground upon which to stand, and was impelled to face social ostracism and bitterest persecution by the conviction that in Jesus Christ alone was to be found that which his heart craved. Of these the first was baptized in 1832, and subsequent years witnessed the acceptance of the Lord Jesus as Saviour, by a not inconsiderable number of the brightest young men of Bengal.

Of these some entered upon missionary work, others upon Government service in their own Province, and still others, by no means few in number, found their life work in distant parts of the country.

Of these last, a larger number migrated to the Panjab than to any other Province. The reason for this is fairly obvious. The years during which the first foundations of the Christian Church were being laid in the new region far to the Northwest, were those in which the first-fruits of the labors of Dr. Duff and his colleagues were most fully becoming manifest in Bengal.

The spiritual fathers of the young Bengali Christians, with a splendid breadth of sympathy for other branches of the Church of Christ, gladly encouraged them to heed the calls to service, which began to come to them from the rapidly opening fields to the North.

Mission schools in Ludhiana, Lahore, Amritsar, Peshawar, Rawalpindi, Multan, Jalandhar, Saharanpur, Dehra, Batala, Gujranwala and Sialkot, all, in fact, of the advanced schools established by the Presbyterian and Church of England Missions to the north and west of Delhi, shared in the helpful labors of these men, who, equipped with such excellent training as the Scottish colleges had given. them in Calcutta, were able to enter at once upon effective service, in a land whose vernaculars, were at the outset, almost entirely unfamiliar to them.

The demand for an English education began to show itself. These men were prepared to supply it, and pupils came in crowds to the schools, where the daily study of the Bible was an established part of the curriculum. Each Christian teacher became a missionary, and it is unquestionably true that the mighty influence exerted by the schools referred to, and by others as well, was largely due to the presence in them, during the first decades of their existence, of men trained at the feet of Dr. Duff, his associates, and their immediate successors.

Some of these entered the Gospel ministry, others spent long and useful lives as teachers. The things God wrought through them cannot be adequately estimated now, and it is no part of the present purpose to attempt to measure them.

Of the life of one of them, this little book will attempt to tell the story. It is a story that deserves to be rehearsed, for it is a testimony to the way in which God can purify and beautify and energize a devoted life. It may also, we trust, serve as a source of encouragement and inspiration to others who are, it may be, in these later days, seeking to discern the will of God with reference to their own lives.

On May 31st, 1916, there passed to his eternal rest, one of India's great sons, Kali Charan Chatterjee; perhaps not great as the world counts greatness; for although he was much esteemed and beloved by thousands in India, Europe and America, and rose to a position of prominence in his own Church, yet the very nature of the service which occupied his life precluded his taking a place amongst those most widely known even in his own country. His life and the secret of its efficiency and power were summed up in the last words uttered by him as surrounded by his family, he calmly awaited the end. That utterance was, "I am a servant of Jesus Christ."

As on the day following that closing scene we stood by his grave in the cemetery at Hoshyarpur, surrounded by a great multitude, some of whom he had led to Christ, and all of whom had gathered to mourn his departure and render their tribute to his memory, all felt afresh something of the extraordinary beauty and usefulness of the life that had been spent so largely and so unselfishly in that great district of the Panjab, where he had founded and led the Christian Church for more than two score years. No adequate picture of a life such as his could possibly be drawn which would leave out of sight the transformations wrought in the lives of thousands who came under the direct and indirect influence of his life.

But before we enter upon any attempt to tell of what he did, let us glance at some of the outstanding facts of his early days, as our best means of understanding in some measure, the character which left so large an impress upon great numbers of people of so many types and such diverse forms of faith.

II

EARLY YEARS

No study of the Veda nor oblation, no gift of alms, nor round of strict observance can lead the inwardly depraved to heaven.—*Laws of Manu ii.* 97.

KALI CHARAN CHATTERJEE was born on August 23d, 1839, at Sukhchar, a village situated on the left bank of the river Hugli, some eight miles north of Calcutta. His father's name was Ram Hari Chatterjee, a Kulin Brahman of the Radhiya class. This class of Brahmans traces its descent from five priests, who are said to have been brought from Kanauj by Raja Adhisar of East Bengal, in the ninth century A.D. Priests competent to perform the Vedic sacrifices could only be found in the capitals of the great Hindu Kings; hence this importation, and the descendants of those who were brought from such a distance are naturally proud of their lineage. The modern forms of the names of the five sections of the Radhiya Brahmans are

Mukerjee; Banerjee; Chatterjee; Ganguli and Ghosal. All are known as Kulin Brahmans, or Brahmans of good family or lineage, and indeed are sometimes designated as the Brahmans of the Brahmans. To this lineage belong such distinguished men of the present day as Mr. W. C. Banerjee, Sir Guru Das Banerjee of Calcutta and the late Sir Protul Chandra Chatterjee of Lahore. The subject of our sketch was thus, as we see, born to a social rank second to none in Hindu Society. During his early years, he was left largely to the charge of an Aunt, his mother's sister, and to her he owed much. His father, as manager of a part of the estate of the Raja of Subha Bazar, was absent from his home a large portion of each year and his mother was obliged to spend much of her time in the management of household affairs.

Throughout life, he loved to speak of the influence exercised upon him in the days of his childhood by his aunt, who, as a widow from her childhood, devoted much of her time to the memorizing of the Shastras, the religious books of her faith, to prayer and to alms-giving. She appears to have taught her young charge to serve the gods, and to have delighted in relating to him many stories of their prowess, as she had gathered them from the Puranas, or the eighteen books of comparatively modern Hinduism, the Ramayana and the Mahabharata, the great epic poems of India, through the recitations of the Pandits.

In the home at Sukhchar, the gods of the Hindu Pantheon were recognized and worshipped; especially the images of Kali,[1] Shiva[2] and Krishna[3] to each of of which was accorded a place in a little temple within the house. As a Sakta, or worshipper of the Sakti, or female counterpart of Shiva, the father of the family was wont to offer goats and occasionally buffaloes before the image of Kali. In a sense it may be said that the children were brought up in a faith in which "without the shedding of blood there is no remission of sins."

At the age of five Kali Charan entered the village school, where he was taught Reading, Writing and Arithmetic. To the end of his life, he was able to repeat a Sanscrit passage from a little book called the Shishubodhak, apparently used as a moral text-book in the school, the substance of which is this, "Regard other people's wives as your mother, other peo-

[1] Or Durga, the consort of Shiva.
[2] The third person of the Hindu Triad.
[3] An incarnation of Vishnu.

ple's things as stones and consider all souls as your own soul."

The most important ceremony in the life of every Hindu lad of the Brahman, Kshatriya and Vaishya castes was performed, in his case, at the age of eight years, when he was invested with the sacred thread, called Upanayana, the symbol of the *Dwija,* or twice-born. The thread, or Yajnopavita, in the case of a Brahman, consists of a cotton cord of three strands, worn over the left shoulder. The cord worn by a Kshatriya is made of hemp, and that worn by a Vaishya of wool. The ritual of initiation to the number of the Twice-Born, as performed in the Brahman family, may be briefly described as follows:

The head of the boy is shaved and his ears pierced with tiny silver pins prepared for this occasion. After this he is bathed and dressed in the garb of a mendicant and caused, while facing the sun, to walk twice around the sacred fire. The officiating priest, by repeating the Gayatri[1] ten times, consecrates the Yajnopavita and places it on the shoulder of the novitiate. After this, he is required to ask alms of each of the assembled company, and is then initiated into the daily use of the Gayatri, and on

[1] A spell of peculiar efficacy.

the morning and evening prayers, or Sandhyas. The ceremony is concluded by the binding on of a girdle of *munja* grass. The Gayatri prayer referred to above, may be freely rendered into English as follows:—"We meditate on the excellent glory of the divine life-giver. May he stimulate our understanding." Other exhortations such as these, which follow, form a part of the ceremony, which we have attempted to describe in outline:—Bathe every day; offer oblations of water to the gods, holy sages and departed ancestors; and neglect not to feed the sacred fire with fuel. Abstain from meat, perfumes, unguents, sensuality, wrath, covetousness, dancing, music, gambling, detraction of others, falsehood, impurity of all kinds, and never injure any being. Never bow your head to make obeisance to one who is not a Brahman. When saluted by a man of a class other than your own, say only, "Victory be unto you! From this day the Brahm dwells in you; keep yourself therefore pure."

In estimating the influences that operated in shaping the ideas and character at the most impressionable period of his life, of such a lad as the one of whom we write, this ceremony of investiture can be given no second place. Long years afterwards, in speaking of the occasion, he referred to the profound impression made upon him by the idea then emphasized that he should renounce the world and consider himself as the "temple of the divine spirit" and that he should abstain from everything low and degrading.

Shortly after the ceremony, just referred to, Kali Charan became a pupil of the Anglo Vernacular High School conducted by the C. M. S. at Agarparah, a distance of some two miles from his father's house. The object in view was that he might learn the English language, but in truth it was there that he acquired his first acquaintance with the Christian Scriptures. The Head Master, Babu Guru Charan Bose, was a man of strong and earnest Christian character, and every one of his nine associates was also a Christian. The exemplary and consistent lives of the Head Master and of one of his assistants, in particular, powerfully influenced many of the pupils. Young Chatterjee, unusually thoughtful for his years, soon began to compare the life and character of the Lord Jesus Christ with those of the gods he had been taught to worship. He spent much time in the reading of the Mahabharata, the Ramayana, and the Puranas; and became greatly interested in contrasting their contents with those of the Bible. As a result of this study he soon arrived at the definite conviction that Jesus is indeed "holy, harmless and undefiled," adopted His precepts and made them the guiding principles of his life.

At about the same time, he won first place in the Scripture examination of the school, and received as a prize, a beautifully bound copy of the Bible. Joining with three fellow students, in the careful reading of this volume and in prayer that God might show them the light and guide them into His Truth, this group of lads early became impressed by such passages as the following:

> "He hath made him to be sin for us, who knew no sin; that we might be made the righteousness of God in Him."
>
> "Who His own Self bare our sins in His own Body on the tree, that we being dead unto sin might live unto righteousness; by whose stripes we are healed."
>
> "He gave His life a ransom for many."

Of this group of seekers after light and the progress made by them, their leader, in after years, left this record:—"Passages like these convinced us that Christ's death and sufferings were vicarious—He died for our sins and in our stead—so that it is not enough to receive Him as our Teacher and Guide, but also as our sin-offering to reconcile us to God. This doctrine became a stumbling block in the path of our progress for a time, and we hesitated to accept it, feeling satisfied to follow Christ as our Guru and Leader. It was not until we carefully considered the 5th Chapter of the Epistle to the Romans, especially the verses twelve and eighteen, that all our hesitation was removed, and we accepted Him in all His fullness as our Teacher and Saviour. We prayed over this discovery and thanked God for it. We determined to make an open profession of our faith in Christ."

The worship of idols was forthwith abandoned, as were also others of the rites and ceremonies of Hinduism, which had now become obnoxious to these young inquirers. But the public declaration of their faith upon which they had resolved, was not yet to be made. Difficulties, which in the first warmth of conviction they had not measured, began to appear as, at least, possible ground for postponement, or even of a final decision to serve as secret disciples.

At about this time a senior student of the school made public profession of faith in Christ and was baptized. A storm of persecution burst upon him. Driven from his home, separated from friends and relatives, he was at once esteemed an outcast from society and was abused and mocked wherever he went. The pressure put upon him was overwhelming, greater than anything that can be easily imagined by those who have not themselves been personal witnesses of such scenes of struggle as not infrequently follow upon a decision to obey the Divine command, at whatever cost. In this case human weakness triumphed, the youth abandoned the struggle, recanted his newly found faith, and returned to Hinduism. This event seriously disturbed the mind of young Chatterjee, and greatly weakened his determination to profess openly his faith. He, not unnaturally, feared that, in the time of testing, he too might fail. The temptation came to him which has assailed many. The suggestion was that he remain a secret disciple, and try to serve God through Christ, though nominally a Hindu. But, in dwelling upon this as a possible way of doing the will of God, he was able to find no rest. The words of Christ could not be driven from his mind, "Whosoever shall confess his sins before men, him will I confess also before my Father in heaven; but whosoever will not confess me before men, him will I not confess before my Father in heaven."

Finally, a conclusion was reached. A public profession of faith was seen to be necessary. Baptism must be received at whatever cost. This was the mind of Christ and it must be fulfilled in a simple dependence upon His grace and power for that help, without which even the strongest would surely fall.

Realizing the serious nature of the many obstacles, which would inevitably confront them in their determination to unite with the Christian Church, were it to be carried into effect at Agarparah, in the midst of acquaintances and relatives, the four young friends resolved, if possible, to migrate from the school, where they had learned so much of the Way of Life, to the Christian College in Calcutta. They knew there were many Christian converts there and expected to receive from them, as well as from Dr. Duff and his colleagues that sympathy and protection of which they were assured that they would shortly stand in sore need. In this expectation, they were not, as we shall later learn, disappointed. Meanwhile, they succeeded in persuading their parents and guardians to consent to their departure for Calcutta, where, in the early part of 1854, they found themselves admitted as regular pupils in the School department of the College.

III

SCHOOL AND COLLEGE DAYS IN CALCUTTA

The tidal wave of deeper souls
Into our inmost being rolls.
—*Longfellow.*

IT was at the time of the Durga Puja festival in the month of October of the year 1854, that Kali Charan took his first open and public step in the direction of separating himself from the social and religious life of his own people. He refused to take any part in the festival, and definitely informed his father of his purpose to become a Christian and to be publicly baptized. To the father the idea seemed so preposterous that, at first, he could not believe in the seriousness of the son's intention. When, however, he came to recognize that the lad had formed a definite purpose, he became greatly troubled and solemnly warned him of the results of the course which he contemplated. Amongst these, his being cast out of his home and ostracised from all his friends and relatives, were perhaps the most conspicuously presented. But none of these things moved him. On the fourth day of the following month, he wrote a letter, which he arranged should be delivered after he had left for school. In this he announced his determination not to return home at the close of the day, but to go to the Free Church Mission House and ask for baptism.

This plan was carried into effect, and, having accompanied some of the Christian students of his classes to the Mission House, he applied for baptism. Dr. Duff, being at the time absent in Scotland, the young man was cordially welcomed by the Rev. Dr. David Ewart, the Superintendent of the Mission, and four days later, i. e. on November 8th, 1854, he was baptized by him in the Free Church situated on Wellesley Street. The relation between the young convert and Dr. Ewart was, from the outset, one of peculiar confidence and affection, and it would be difficult to overestimate the influence of that close association upon the long life and work of the young man whose mind and heart were then being prepared for the struggles and victories of later years.

During the past three or four scores of

years remarkable changes have been witnessed in the attitude of the people of India toward caste and all that the system involves in its relation to the individual Hindu. The spread of education, the introduction of new facilities for travel and communication, the increasing frequency of visits to Europe and America, together with the growth of independent thought and action, have served to loosen, in some measure, the bonds which, for long centuries, had held in subjection the entire Hindu people. This relaxation of caste rules has been much more rapid in its operation in Northwestern India than elsewhere; nevertheless the process of emancipation is visible throughout the country. In the days of Kali Charan Chatterjee's boyhood, the people of Bengal, with the exception of the very few, neither shared in nor desired such emancipation. To the Bengalis pollution of caste was dangerous, not only to the one guilty of its violation, but to all the members of his family as well, dead, living and unborn, and in less degree to other members of his caste.

The very thought of stepping beyond caste regulations and becoming thus numbered amongst the base-born, and those destined to everlasting, hopeless degradation and misery, must have caused the lad to shrink in horror from such a course, when it was first suggested to him. In after life it was not his wont to speak much of the things which he had been called upon to suffer. He came to regard them as of exceeding small importance when weighed against what he had obtained in Christ, and yet we know he literally gave up all as soon as he heard the call. His relations and friends cast him out from home, and regarded him as dead and worse, for had he not brought disgrace upon them all? Every purely worldly and human consideration would have led him to determine upon a life of hidden discipleship. But in the face of all obstacles and dangers faith triumphed and gave him a victory which was the beginning of a long line of triumphs extending through his splendidly fruitful life.

Cast out by parents and other relatives and friends, some twenty young students found, at that time, a home in a hostel erected in a Compound where was also situated the house in which Dr. Duff lived. Of this hostel Rev. Lal Behari Day was Superintendent. Here for full seven years, young Chatterjee lived the life of a student and found these among the happiest years of his life. The routine of each day was regulated by a program drawn up in Dr. Duff's own hand. The Sunday schedule was this: From 7 to 8 A. M. a Bible Class, taught by Dr. Duff. 11 A. M. Public worship in English. 4 to 5 P. M. a class in which the Shorter Catechism was taught and reports of missionary work in several parts of the world read. At 6 P. M. Public worship in Bengali was conducted by Dr. Ewart. In addition to this. a portion of each week day was devoted to the careful training of the Christian students. But even more than this, stress appears to have been laid, by the members of the Staff, upon that most important feature of a Christian education, namely, definite training in character, through close personal contact between pupil and teacher. The constant care and influence of such men as Dr. Ewart, Rev. Lal Behari Day and Dr. Duff, bore great fruit in the lives of those for whom it was their joy to labor. Were it to be asked which of the two, personal contact with Christian men, or the direct study of the Christian Scriptures, was the more powerful force in the development of the spiritual life of their pupils, no very satisfactory or perfectly discriminating answer could probably be given. But that an intellectual conviction of the truth and reasonableness of the Christian Scriptures bore an important share in the process that led these young men into the full light of faith, cannot be doubted. Statements as to the part played by doctrinal teaching in the lives of the converts of that day, are not lacking in the auto-biographical notes left by many of them. Such notes made by Kali Charan are worthy of being reproduced at some length.

"It has been often asked why I renounced Hinduism and became a disciple of Christ. My answer is, that I was drawn almost unconsciously to Christ by His holy and blameless life, his devotion to the will of God and His works of mercy and benevolence toward suffering humanity. The excellence of His precepts as given in the "Sermon on the Mount" and His love for sinners won my admiration and my heart. I admired and loved Him. The incarnations I had been taught to worship, Rama, Krishna, Mahadeo and Kali were all incarnations of power—they were heroes, sinful men of like passions with ourselves. Christ only appeared to me as holy and worthy to be adored as God. But the doctrine which decided me to embrace the Christian religion and make a public profession of my faith, was the doctrine of the vicarious death and sufferings of Christ. I felt myself a sinner and found in Christ one who had died for my sins—paid the penalty due to my sins 'For by grace are ye saved through faith, and that not of yourselves, it is the gift of God.' 'Not of works lest any man should boast.' This was the burden of the thought of my heart, Christ has died, and, in doing so, paid a debt which man could never pay. This conviction which has grown stronger and stronger with my growth in Christian life and experience has now (1910) become a part of my life. It is the differentiating line between Christianity and all other religions. I felt it so when I became a Christian, and feel it most strongly now. 'A God all mercy is a God unjust' continues to be my creed to this day."

The school and college career of our young student was of a most creditable description. From the school he passed into the college, two years after leaving school at Agarparah. His ability and diligence, during those years, were marked by his being awarded two silver medals, one for the best essay on female education, and the other for being head of the school. Again in the Entrance examination, he took a place sufficiently high to secure for him a scholarship of Rs. 8 per mensem for the first two years of his College course. While in College, he gained still further distinctions and certain emoluments connected with them. Among these may be mentioned, a silver medal for the best essay on "The Best Mode of Carrying on Female Education," a prize for the best essay on "The Social Characteristics of the Mahrattas"; the Hawkins Theological Scholarship of Rs. 8 a month for two years, a Mathematical prize for the best solutions of one hundred problems in Conic Sections; and still another for the highest proficiency in English History. He was also selected as a teacher of English Literature in the Entrance class of the School, a position which he held until the time arrived when he was to leave Calcutta.

There were great men and great teachers in the Free Church College. Dr. Duff taught such subjects as Logic, Metaphysics, Moral Philosophy and Evidences of Christianity, together with certain of the Masters of English Literature. Dr. Mackay was a great astronomer; Dr. Smith a distinguished mathematician, and Dr. David Ewart, who appears to have been a man capable of giving instruction in a variety of subjects, taught such as English, Mathematics, and History. He has been described as the very soul of the institution. An incessant worker, he was wont to arrive at the College at 10 A. M. daily, and usually to remain there busily occupied until 5 P. M. One who knew him, as a man and teacher, without any thought of ascribing any less of credit to the great Duff than was his due, indeed he spoke of him as the outstanding teacher and organizer of the institution, in referring to Ewart and Duff, said that the conception of the College was Dr. Duff's; but the carrying out of that conception was Dr. Ewart's task.

In October, 1860, this great teacher was stricken down by Cholera. The entire student community was profoundly stirred. A group of Christian young men spent the night preceding the funeral, by the body of the honored dead. It was to them a most solemn occasion, one on which more than one of them in the darkness of the night, in the presence of the dead, after earnest heart searching and prayer, solemnly dedicated themselves to the service of Christ. This was the first formal dedication, on the part of Kali Charan, of his life to missionary service. The solemn vow then taken, in memory of the beloved preceptor and pastor, who had just left him, was never, throughout the long life that followed, forgotten. Before the vow was made, God's Spirit seemed to impress upon his mind and heart words which he loved to quote as the basis and encouragement for all effort to win men to Christ, "Ye are not your own. For ye are bought with a price; therefore glorify God in your body and in your spirit, which are God's."

We have now reached a point where, in order that we may appreciate the causes which led to his leaving Calcutta and setting his face toward what seemed like a foreign land, reference must be made to an unpleasant difference which arose between three ordained Indian ministers of the Free Church and the foreign members of the Presbytery. These Indian brethren, basing their claim upon the doctrine of the parity of the ministry, asked that they be given equality of position and authority with the Foreign Missionaries in the Mission Council, and in the administration of all Mission work. They claimed that this parity not only existed in ecclesiastical courts, but also in the work of the Church and that they ought to be made full members of the Mission, with a seat and a vote in the Mission Council.

In this controversy all the Christian students sympathized keenly with the Indian ministers and considered the Mission as unjust in its attitude toward them. No one felt this more deeply than Kali Charan Chatterjee and he resolved that, if an opportunity presented itself for him to leave the Mission, and work in connection with some other Society, he would avail himself of it. Little did he then know that the same anomalous conditions existed in all Missionary societies. However, he determined that, if in other societies, the privileges for which his ordained brethren were asking, should be refused he would try to find a place for himself in the subordinate position of a teacher.

In a subsequent chapter of this biography it is hoped that there may be found space for some brief reference to his personal attitude on this question of the relation of the Indian clergy to the authoritative administration of the affairs of the Mission or Council. Meanwhile it is both interesting and instructive to note, as we do, that important movements or currents in the Church of Christ in India, took their rise from this serious divergence in opinion between brethren concerning whose devotion to the cause of Christ, none who knew them, could entertain the slightest doubt.

It was in the month of October, 1861, that a letter was received by Mr. Chatterjee from the Rev. Golaknath, of Jalandhar, in the Panjab, offering him the position of Headmaster of the Mission School there, and inviting him to become a co-worker in the service of Christ, in the department of education. The young man was pleased and thankful to receive such an invitation, and after much prayerful consideration, he was led to conclude that the call was from God. He accepted it and, with little delay, set out upon his long journey to his new field beyond the Sutlej.

IV.

EARLIER YEARS IN THE PANJAB

"This one thing I do."

ARRIVING in Jalandhar on November 21st, 1861, the young, ardent and well equipped teacher entered upon his work in the Mission School. It was then that he became connected with the Church and Mission in which the remaining years of his long and devoted life were to be spent. This separation from the Church in which he had been taught and in which he had made public profession of his faith in Christ, he did not regard lightly, even though the change consisted in nothing more than a transference of relationship from one administrative organization to another. The organization with which he now became connected was, in its ecclesiastical nature, identical with that in which he had received his earlier nurture. A member of the Presbyterian Church in Calcutta, his connection was with the Free Church of Scotland; as a member of the Presbyterian Church in the Panjab, his special relationship was with the Presbyterian Church in the U. S. A. Unimportant as this change in relationship might appear, it nevertheless involved a severance of old ties and was to him a very real trial. Yet, when long years afterwards, he was honored by his brethren of the Presbyterian Church in India, by being chosen as its first Moderator, the old pain had surely all disappeared and been supplanted by a very lively satisfaction and thanksgiving in recognition of the fact that, through the labors of himself and others, barriers that had no right to find a place between Christian workers of substantially the same convictions, had begun to fall.

From the very outset, his work at Jalandhar seems to have given great satisfaction; the school grew in numbers and in efficiency, and attention was drawn to him from many quarters. During the years 1861-1864 the School was developed into an Anglo-Vernacular School, teaching up to the Entrance Standard. The first Entrance examination ever held in the Panjab took place in 1865. Four young men of the Jalandhar School were sent up to this test, of whom two were successful. It is of interest to note that, of these two, one was the late George Solomon Lewis, who in later years, was distinguished as a member of the Provincial Civil Service, and, throughout his life, as a man of God and a power for good in the several posts of influence which he held in various parts of the Province.

It was as has been seen, through the Rev. Mr. Golaknath, the first Brahman convert of the American Presbyterian Church in India, that Mr. Chatterjee found a sphere for the beginning of his service in the Panjab. Mr. Golaknath was for many years in charge of the work of the Mission at Jalandhar and exercised an extraordinary influence throughout the whole region of country lying between the Sutlej and the Beas rivers. On June 6th, 1862, Mr. Chatterjee was united in marriage to Mary, the second daughter of Mr. and Mrs. Golaknath; and then began a life of wonderfully blessed service rendered by this devoted pair which extended over a period of fifty-four years.

Their family consisted of one son and four daughters. Golaknath, the son, after a brilliant career as a student in India and in the University of Cambridge, was appointed a Professor of Mathematics in the Government College, Lahore, where after a score or more

Dr. Chatterjee in 1887, while on a visit to the United States at the invitation of the Presbyterian Board of Missions.

years of admirable service, he died some years ago. During a portion of this period, he was one of the Directors of the Forman Christian College.

Mona, the eldest daughter, became the wife of Dr. D. N. P. Datta, then a Civil Surgeon —and now a Medical missionary. She too was called from earth some years ago. In her memory a beautiful Church building, known as the "Mona Memorial," was erected for the use of the congregation at Hoshyarpur.

The second daughter, Lena, after a number of years of active service as a missionary along with her parents in Hoshyarpur, was married to Kanwar Raghbir Singh, son of Raja Sir and Rani Lady Harnam Singh, a member of the Panjab Service.

The third daughter, Nina, is the wife of Dr. George Nundy of the Hyderabad State service.

The youngest member of this exceedingly interesting group of children, Dora, was partly educated in the United States, where she graduated in medicine. For a number of years thereafter she was a physician in charge of the Denny Hospital for Women at Hoshyarpur, and rendered most admirable service as a colleague in the missionary work of the Station, of her parents and sister. Later she became the wife of Rai Sahib Manghat Rai, B.A., a member of the provincial Civil Service in the Northwest Frontier Province.

Shortly after his marriage, Mr. Chatterjee was offered by the Head of the Government Educational department, the post of Headmaster in such schools as those at Gujranwala and Hoshyarpur. These were tempting offers. The work proposed was lucrative, with prospect of promotion, and, after a period of years, a pension. Both offers were, however, firmly declined upon the ground that he had resolved to serve God as a Christian teacher or preacher, as opportunity might come to him.

His salary as a Mission School teacher was small. An incident connected with one of the offers of Government Service just referred to deserves more than casual mention.

When the offer was made, it was fully discussed, and finally Mr. and Mrs. Chatterjee decided to accept it. They reasoned in this way, that in a new post of service, they would continue to let their light shine and would do everything they could to promote their Redeemer's Kingdom. They accepted the post and made arrangements to leave. The last day arrived and the gari stood before the door. Trunks and boxes had been placed on top of the vehicle and they were ready to leave their old home and their work in the Mission for good. At the last moment, Mrs. Chatterjee said, "I am not yet satisfied. Let us go back into the house and pray about it again." They went back and knelt down in their dismantled home. They prayed unitedly for guidance, and, when they arose from their knees, they both said with one accord, "We will not go. God has placed us here. God has planted us in this place and in this work that we should bring forth fruit for Him. He will provide. We will trust and not be afraid." So the boxes were unloaded and the gari sent away, the old home put in order ȃgain and the old work went on. The verse which sums up the experience of Mr. and Mrs. Chatterjee at that time and throughout the years is this, "Except a grain of wheat fall into the ground and die it remaineth alone; but if it die, it beareth much fruit." How wonderfully the confidence of Mr. and Mrs. Chatterjee in God was justified. At the moment of self-dedication, they died to all human ambition and made the great venture of faith. This is the secret of their wonderful fruitfulness in the Master's work.

In the year 1849, the year of the annexation of the Panjab to the British Empire, the Rev.

John Newton and the Rev. C. W. Forman, of the Presbyterian Mission, opened work in Lahore, the capital city of the Province. A school was at once founded, which speedily became a source of tremendous influence throughout the entire region. It would be difficult to overestimate the part borne by that institution in shaping the lives and characters of thousands of youths, who, especially in the early days of British occupancy, when, at the outset, the large majority of English-educated employees of Government had to be found from amongst the students of the great Mission School.

In December, 1865, it was resolved to open College classes in connection with the School, and this was done in the following year. The Rev. C. W. Forman was at the head of both the School and College departments and Mr. Chatterjee was offered and accepted the post of Junior Professor of mathematics. It might appear that his future career had thus been determined by circumstances, and that his life was to be devoted to the work of teaching. But previous to this call to the College, there had come another call, to which he felt he dared not turn a deaf ear. He was wont to describe it as "God's call to me to enter the

Gospel Ministry," and to declare that, when it came, old objections entirely disappeared, and that he resolved never again to think, in so far as it concerned himself, of the matter of inequality of position between Indian and American missionaries, in the administration of Mission work. His desire to be set apart for the Ministry was communicated to the Presbytery, and in November, 1864, he was accepted as a candidate. By direction of this body, he pursued his studies in Theology and Church History, under the guidance of the Rev. John Newton and the Rev Golaknath, and, in New Testament Greek, under that of Rev. W. J. P. Morrison. After the satisfactory completion of all his trial examinations, he was licensed to preach the Gospel in December, 1867, and on December 24th of the following year, was solemnly ordained to the ministry of the Gospel by the Presbytery of Ludhiana, at its meeting at Ludhiana.

From January, 1866, until March, 1868, Mr. and Mrs. Chatterjee devoted their energies to work in Lahore, he to teaching in the School and College classes and to Bazaar Preaching, and she to visiting and teaching the ladies in some of the Bengali families in the City.

His teaching duties included the teaching of

Mathematics to the First and Second Year classes and also to the Entrance class; Logic and Philosophy to the Third and Fourth Year classes, and also Scripture to one of the classes. For a time he acted as Headmaster of the School. Sixteen out of the twenty-four hours of each day did not seem to him too much to devote to active work and preparation for it. Those years were to him years of great joy in the service which he was enabled to perform, and the period was a time, too, during which he felt that he gained much by way of preparation for the years that were to follow. He esteemed his association with Mr. Newton and Mr. Forman an exceedingly great privilege. He gained their fullest confidence; they loved and trusted him, and he loved and honored them. He aimed to carry out their wishes and they, in turn, soon came to esteem him as, in all respects, worthy, and capable to take the fullest share, with them, in all the affairs of the Mission Station. The mutual friendship, love and confidence which had its beginning then, continued, in a remarkable degree, to exist among these men of God as long as their lives lasted. This fellowship of kindred spirits was undoubtedly a powerful influence in shaping the life of the youngest of the three, as he shortly entered upon a new sphere, where new and untried burdens had to be borne, and new problems to be faced and dealt with.

At the Annual Meeting of the Ludhiana (now Panjab) Mission, held in 1866 a letter from Mr. H. E. Perkins, Deputy Commissioner of Hoshyarpur, was read, in which he suggested that the Mission establish work at that place. In response to this request, it was resolved that Hoshyarpur be taken up as a sub-station of Lahore, subject to the approval of the Board in New York, and that Rev. Guru Das Moitra be appointed to begin work in that place. The approval of the Board having been received, Mr. Moitra proceeded to the new station; but within a few months after his arrival, he fell seriously ill, and was compelled to seek a change of scene in order to recruit his health. Domestic affliction of a most trying character followed upon his illness, and so at the end of the year 1867, he was recalled to his former position, at the Rang Mahal School, Lahore.

At this juncture, it became clear to the Mission, that for the great new field at Hoshyarpur, God had provided, in the persons of Mr. and Mrs. Chatterjee, those who could be sent into it, with the utmost confidence, and with great expectation of an abundant harvest. We know how amply the years that followed justified that decision.

The invitation came to them early in 1868. They felt it to be a summons not from the Mission only, but from God himself. They arrived on March 4th, 1868, and they came, to use his own words, "fully consecrating themselves, their bodies and souls, to the Saviour of mankind being determined 'to know nothing but Christ and Him crucified,' and imploring the blessing of God upon the work."

V

BEGINNINGS IN HOSHYARPUR

Blessed is he who has found his work,
Let him ask no other blessedness.
—*Carlyle.*

THE territory for the evangelization of which the Ludhiana Mission became, at the time, in a sense responsible, comprises an area of 2232 square miles.

It is one of the most populous districts in the Province, having more than 900,000 inhabitants, these being distributed throughout 11 towns and 2117 villages.

Regarding the natural features of this district, its rivers, the Sutlej and the Beas, which bound it on the north and south; its great Chohs, or sandy waterways, which lead into the rivers and intersect great portions of the plains; its Chhambs, or stretches of marshy land; its products and its climate, much might be said. It may be indeed said that, in order to appreciate very adequately the nature of the task that awaited the Missionary in 1868 one should be, to some degree, at least, familiar with these things, as well as with the character of the population, its social condition, and its religious convictions and practices. But obviously this is not the place in which to attempt any detailed description of them. References to certain facts or numbers may indeed be found necessary from time to time; but such will be made only by way of illustrating the nature and progress of the task undertaken and carried forward by the missionaries and will be given in as concise form as may be possible.

With respect to religious affiliations, the population consists of Hindus, Mohammedans, Sikhs, Christians, Jains and a few others.

Amongst those commonly included amongst the Hindus, Mohammedans and Sikhs in census reports are the "Depressed classes" known as the Chuhras, of whom there were 19,205 in 1901, and the Chamars numbering 121,003. A fact that is not without interest is that at the same time, there were enumerated in the dictrict no less than 19,075 mendicant faqirs, the greater number of them being of the Mohammedan faith.

As Mr. and Mrs. Chatterjee entered upon the tremendous task of bringing the knowledge of the Gospel of the Son of God to so heterogeneous a population, spread over so vast a territory, and realized the smallness of their force and the inadequacy of their financial equipment, it is not surprising that they should have paused to carefully deliberate, along with their advisers in their own Mission and with Mr. Perkins, upon whose invitation the station had been opened, as to the agencies to be employed. The conclusions reached by them and the considerations which led to them, were expressed in a very convincing form, in a paper written but a few years ago. It is of interest to remember, in this connection, that the account is written in the light of an experience of more than two score years, and with an obvious assurance that, in adopting the method described, they had been clearly guided by the Spirit of God.

"When I came here, I was an enthusiastic admirer of Missionary education and considered it the most efficient means of extending the Kingdom of Christ and building up His Church in the land, and no wonder that I did so. I was brought to know and love the Saviour through Missionary education and spent the first six years of my service, in the Ludhiana Mission, in educational work. All my antecedents were educational. Yet, after consulting Mr. Perkins, the founder of this Mission, and carefully and prayerfully considering all the circumstances of our new sphere of labor, and especially the very limited force at our command, we concluded to devote the greatest part of our time to the simple preaching of the Gospel and to the distribution of Scriptures and tracts. The only educational work we decided to take up was female education. This was entirely neglected in the district. There was not a single girl's school throughout the length and breadth of the district. Looking back on the decision, after forty-one years, we feel that we were guided to it by the Spirit of God, whose blessings accompanied all our work. With this decision, the work was organized as follows:

1. Daily open air preaching from the veranda of the Reading Room.
2. Evangelistic services three times a week in the City Chapel.
3. Daily conferences with visitors on religious subjects in the Reading Room.
4. Bible class in the Mission House during the summer months.
5. Preaching in religious Melas in the city and its neighborhood.
6. Preaching in the villages by means of winter itineration.
7. Two day schools for Hindu and Mohammedan girls.

"These agencies have been most persistently, prayerfully, and with faith in the word and promises of God made use of for the last forty-one years. They are not opposed to, or disconnected with each other but are mutually helpful and dependent, and form the parts of a connected whole. By means of open air preaching, from the veranda of the Reading Room, we simply proclaim the Gospel Message to passers-by in the street. The audience is fluctuating and often inattentive and noisy. The few, who are impressed, come to the Reading Room and have conferences with the preacher who removes their difficulties and objections, and counsels them as to the right way of enquiry. The evangelistic services in the chapel are conducted with music and singing and exhortation from the word of God. There is no controversy held and the audience is most orderly and attentive, and under the control of the preacher. The Bible Class is meant for more serious enquirers, and has been the means of leading many to Christ. The preaching in melas has the character of open air preaching from the veranda of the Reading Room. In winter itinerations, in the villages, there is always open air preaching and conferences with enquirers at resting places.

"We have tried to combine the above agencies with works of benevolence and personal influence. With this object, we started a poor-house in the City in 1870, and supported it with subscriptions from the Christian residents of the station and grants from Municipal funds. This institution was under my immediate control up to 1891, and has been the means of feeding and clothing thousands of the indigent population in the district. Several thousands have also been supplied with blankets to make them warm in the cold season. Quinine has also been distributed to the sick through us, and we have been able to do all this through the generosity of Christian people. In 1888 the Girl's Orphanage and Boarding School was opened to afford shelter to the homeless and destitute orphans of all Castes and Creeds, to educate them and fit them for the duties and responsibilities of life. In 1902 was opened the Denny Hospital for the relief of pain and suffering amongst women and children. It was with this object also, i. e., of doing good, that I accepted a seat in the Municipal Committee in 1874, and afterwards, when local self-government was introduced, the Presidentship of the same. This brought me into closer contact with the city people and gave me an opportunity of controlling their schools, dispensaries, hospitals and other benevolent institutions, and of generally looking after the comforts of the poor. It was only when my proper work extended to the villages, and I could not do justice to both, that I resigned my connection with the Municipality. It has been our humble endeavor to bring our personal influence to bear upon all with whom we have to come in contact and of allowing no opportunity of doing good to pass away unimproved. Our Saviour's commission to His Apostles was, 'Preach, saying, the Kingdom of Heaven is at hand. Heal the sick, cleanse the lepers, raise the dead, cast out devils. Freely ye have received freely give.' We have tried to work on these lines.

"It may be asked, 'What is the result of our work?"

"My reply is this. The first six years we spent in sowing seed—in preaching the gospel throughout the length and breadth of the land. During this period there were many enquirers and attentive listeners, but only one convert. Hakim Singh, a Hindu Jat from Hukumatpur, declared his faith in Christ and publicly received baptism. At the end of 1873, a general awakening took place among our hearers, a manifestation of God's free grace and the working of His Spirit, and this awakening lasted for nearly ten years. It began at Ghorawaha, and soon extended to Bulowal, and from there to Gardhiwala, Chack, Hoshyarpur and Bhowra. In the course of it, hundreds came forward and confessed Christ to be the only Saviour of men. Twenty-nine families of respectable Hindus and Mohammedans received baptism and joined the Christian Church. Many of them are still alive, adorning different spheres of Christian life and usefulness. The man who took a lead in this movement is still living and is the prosperous head of his village and an elder in the Church. Six devoted themselves to the Gospel Ministry. One of these died a few years ago after a short career of distinguished service. Four are still working as evangelists in this district and the sixth is an influential pastor of one of the Churches of the district of Jalandhar. Three are preaching the Gospel as Licentiates and two are engaged in the humbler work of Catechists.

"Christianity was in great favor with men in those days, and a special unction of the Spirit was given to the preacher, so that, wherever he went, he spoke with power and the Word of God prospered in his hands. Non-Christian people were sometimes afraid to come near him for fear of being drawn away from their faith to Christ."

In this brief statement, we have only the barest outline of the most conspicuous features of the first decade of the history of Hoshyarpur Station. The movement which had its beginning at Ghorawaha, and which resulted in a large ingathering to the Church, beginning from 1873, and lasting almost a decade, was regarded, at the time, as unique in the Panjab, and may indeed be so esteemed. In later years great communal movements have been seen but these have been from amongst the people of the lower classes. As will appear, in the case of some of these movements, there has not always been an entire absence of possible worldly inducement to become identified with the religion of Christ; but in this movement, of which we now speak, there was not only an absence of all such inducements, but the inevitable endurance of severe persecution by everyone who dared to forsake his former faith and publicly identify himself with the Christians. Usually, in such conditions, individuals have entered the Church in small numbers and at long intervals. In the case of the Hoshyarpur ingathering, men and women of good social position came in considerable numbers, at the cost of property and good name among their fellows, and deliberately took up their cross and followed Him. Enough has been said above concerning their life and character to make it abundantly evident that the work was a work of God's Spirit. The present writer came into close personal touch with a number of these converts during the period when they were in course of preparation for the Gospel Ministry and can testify to the things which some of them gladly suffered for Christ's sake and to the beauty of some of the lives which, thank God, are still spared to serve in His Church.

Throughout the first fifteen years following the inception of the work in City and district, Mr. Chatterjee seems to have been an indefatigable itinerant; not that he was ever other than active and diligent in reaching out to the regions beyond the established stations of his district, but it was during the earlier years that he was best able to be, for long periods, absent from the central station. As time passed, responsibilities connected with the supervision of the entire field and with the activities of the main station, together with increasingly heavy burdens, growing out of the position which he had come to occupy in the Church at large, made it difficult or even impossible for him to devote so large a portion of his days to the visitation of remote villages, as he had been able to do in the beginning. And yet we doubt if another Missionary could be mentioned who knew his field, its condition, the quality of his assistants, the fruitfulness or barrenness of particular localities, more thoroughly than he.

In the days of his greatest vigor, when his body was able to keep pace with the increasing longing to make known the riches of the Gospel message, to the tens of thousands, who without him, would never, humanly speaking, have an opportunity of hearing it, we think of him as incessantly active in carrying the truth to remote religious Melas, at such shrines as Chintpurni, Garhdiwala, Dharamkot, and Rajni at Jhaggi and Anandpur. Here (Anandpur) Guru Govind Singh was born and brought up, and here, for the first time, he administered the ceremony of Pahal (Sikh Baptism) to his disciples in the temple of Kesgarh. There are several splendidly built temples here and at Kirtpur, nearby. A great Mela is held here annually, at the time of the Holi festival. It was in one of these Melas that the Rev. Levi Janvier, of the Presbyterian Mission was killed by a Sikh fanatic in 1864. (It will be of interest to some to know that Mr. Janvier was the father of Rev. C. A. R. Janvier, D.D., President of the Ewing Christian College at Allahabad.)

By the end of what may be loosely indicated as the first fifteen years of his ministry in Hoshyarpur, much had been accomplished. He had studied that great field of ninety miles in length and thirty miles in breadth. To a remarkable degree, he had come to know the people of all classes and they to know him. From amongst them, small groups of believers had been gathered; misunderstandings as to the motives of the missionary had been removed; a corps of Christian helpers had been organized; and arrangements made for the regular preaching of the Word and the shepherding of the people in the chief towns of the District. As yet there had been little, if any, manifestation of that movement, which, in more recent years has been associated with great ingatherings to the Church, from the "Depressed classes." Concerning this movement, the manner in which it was met and utilized and its results, we shall speak in another chapter.

VI

WORK AMONG THE LOWLY

"He came not to be ministered unto, but to minister."

THE turning of a multitude to the Lord from amongst the "Depressed classes" in a particular district, cannot be better described than in the language of the Missionary who was himself in the position of leader and guide of all the activities of the Church in that region, at a time when great numbers began to seek admission to it. Fortunately it is possible to insert here a remarkably clear and thoughtful statement from the pen of the Missionary, written after many years of experience had qualified him to estimate the opportunity of the time and to appreciate the importance of this particular form of work, in its relation to the establishing of the kingdom in India. Let it be remembered here that this is the judgment of one who was himself a Brahman, one who, as a Hindu, could have nothing but contempt and loathing for the people of whom he now speaks. He says:

"I shall now say a few words about the work of the Holy Spirit amongst the low class, known as Chuhras:

They belong to the impure class of sweepers and scavengers of towns and cities. In the villages, they are employed as farm-laborers and in making and burning bricks. They are illiterate and sunk in degradation and vice. They have no fixed religion. Those of them who live in Hindu villages, follow the religious customs and manners of the Hindus and give offerings to Hindu gods and goddesses. The Chuhras of Mohammedan villages follow Mohammedan customs. They have no organized priesthood nor sacred books. They worship a saint called Bala Shah. Hindus and Mohammedans look down upon them, and avoid physical contact with them. The number of these people in this district, according to the last census, was 19,205.

The Mass movement amongst these people towards Christianity was not sudden. The first man was baptized in 1888. He was a good man and opened the door for our work among his people and we put our greatest force on it. At first the baptisms were by units, then by tens and hundreds, and at last, by thousands, and even whole villages came forward and asked to be enrolled in the Christian Church. Our experience in connection with this work is as follows:

1. We believe it to have been caused by a special providence of God's grace, and the working of His Spirit. It has not been peculiar among the Chuhras of this district, but has extended to

the whole province and the whole of North India. Similar movements have taken place in South India also. God has His times of special visitations of grace for special peoples, and I believe the Mass Movement amongst the Chuhras of this district to be one of them. We believe it also to have been caused by the steady and faithful work of God's people amongst them. Amongst the minor causes may be mentioned the freedom from religion and social restraint enjoyed by these people, and the ease with which they could accept new truths. Besides they had nothing to lose, but everything to gain by becoming Christians. Many of those, who are influenced by this movement, become Christians from the love of truth, and to satisfy the spiritual instincts and yearnings of their souls. Some come to simply raise themselves in social status, and to enjoy the advantages of education offered to their children by the Mission, and others without thinking of any special objects, join their brethren without any special aim. Thus they are influenced by various motives.

2. The best mode of dealing with them is to receive them all and carry them through a course of instruction, and inform them of the objects of Christianity and, when they are sufficiently improved, and able to make an intelligent and creditable profession of their new faith, and show signs of real penitence, by giving up idolatrous and other sinful practices, they should be baptized. There should not be "Mass-baptisms" in "Mass-movements." Every case of application should be decided on its own merits. This seems to me to be the wisest and safest course.

3. I believe the movement in our district to

be genuine, to be from God and a sincere desire, on the part of these people, to embrace the Christian religion. To make it permanent and productive of spiritual fruitfulness, the work should be followed up by daily pastoral care and teaching and by bringing our own personal influence to bear on them, to bring them up in the life and faith of Christ. Efforts should be also made to educate their children, and to teach them some clean and more respectable industry or trade.

One racial characteristic of these people is their dullness of understanding. What you teach them today they forget tomorrow. Heredity and ignorance from time immemorial have made them dull. Great patience and perseverance are necessary to overcome this difficulty. They should be taught line upon line; precept upon precept, and that by the word of mouth.

A second characteristic is their want of moral apprehension. In many cases the conscience has to be created anew, and in all enlightened. Heredity and ignorance of all right and wrong for generations has deadened their conscience and destroyed all, or nearly all, moral sensibility. Patient and prayerful working is necessary to restore life and light to the newcomers.

4. Admission of Chuhras into the Christian Church lowered its social and moral status in the eyes of the Hindus for a time. But it soon became evident to them that our object was not to become Chuhras, but to raise them from their present degraded and depressed condition."

At the time of Dr. Chatterjee's retirement from the active supervision of the District work of Hoshyarpur, the Christian Community numbered 3106 persons, scattered throughout 118 villages. These had been organized into five churches, with the following numerical strength:

I. *The Hoshyarpur Church.*

1. Number of baptized members....566
2. Number of Communicants....... 98
3. Number of Catechumens 150

II. *The Ghorawaha Church.*

1. Number of baptized members....336
2. Number of Communicants.......115
3. Number of Catechumens 280

III. *The Tanda Church.*

1. Number of baptized members....730
2. Number of Communicants.......474
3. Number of Catechumens 35

IV. *The Dosuah Church.*

1. Number of baptized members....816
2. Number of Communicants.......730
3. Number of Catechumens 441

V. *The Mukerian Church.*

1. Number of baptized members....924
2. Number of Communicants.......728
3. Number of Catechumens 622

Total.

3106 Baptized Christians.
1939 Communicants.
1528 Catechumens.

No account of the agencies and influences set in operation for the evangelization of that great district would be, in any way, complete, which failed to make mention of the efforts made for the enlightenment and evangelization of women and girls. Again we turn to the words of the Reports, presented to the Mission and Board from year to year, and to a summary penned but five years ago:

"Our educational work has been very limited. We began with two day schools—one for Hindu and another for Mohammedan girls. They were opened in 1869. The latter was more flourishing than the former, but soon collapsed on account of the opposition of the Mohammedans to the teaching of the Scriptures. The former continued for thirty-nine years. It was taught and superintended at first, by Mrs. Chatterjee and afterwards by her two daughters in succession, Miss Mona Chatterjee, and Miss Lena Chatterjee, and only closed on the marriage of the latter, in December, 1907. It was a primary school, teaching reading, writing, arithmetic and embroidery, with the addition of Scripture lessons. The number of girls attending it was forty to fifty every year. Though elementary in character, this school was the center of life and light to many of the homes in the City of Hoshyarpur and the only means at our command of reaching the higher class Hindu women with Christian teaching and influence.

"The Girls' Orphanage and Boarding School has been the other educational institution of this station. It was opened in July, 1888, and the object of opening it was thus explained in the annual report of that year:

"'The object of this institution is not to rival the Girls' Boarding School in Dehra, or the Christian Girls' School in Lahore, or the Alexander School in Amritsar, but to act as a supplement to them. These are meant for the daughters of Indian Christian gentlemen, and give education suited to them. Our school is intended to give home and Christian education to orphan girls, and to the children of the poorer classes of Christians, suited to their state and condition of life.'

"Keeping this end in view, we have tried to bring up the children committed to our care for the last twenty-one years with simple and inexpensive habits, and with careful instruction in the Bible and in secular knowledge, up to the upper Primary Standard. Industries suited to girls, such as housekeeping, cooking, plain and fancy needle-work have also been taught. On an average, five girls have been passed out of this school every year, after finishing the prescribed course. Some of these have been married to Evangelists, Licentiates and Catechists of our Mission, and are taking part with credit in their husbands' work of spreading the Gospel of Christ. Others are married to men in secular occupations and are proving worthy help-meets to their husbands. In our estimation, the school has been a boon, not only to orphan and destitute girls, but also to the poorer Native Christians of our community.

"The school is the result of Mrs. Chatterjee's visit to America in 1887, and may be considered 'a memorial' of it. The Churches in that country asked her to mention some specific object in which they could take interest and give her help to carry it on. She proposed this joint object of a Girls' Orphanage and boarding school for the daughters of the poorer native Christians. The idea struck them as worthy of sympathy and support, and they generously supplied the sum of five thousand dollars, as the first instalment of their gift. On Mrs. Chatterjee's return from America, a suitable site, in a healthy and pleasant part of the station, with a grant from the District Board and contributions from friends in India, was selected. The necessary buildings were put up with the contributions from America, and the work was started in the midst of much encouragement and hope.

"In September, 1900, forty orphans were admitted into the orphanage. Six of them were in the lowest condition of health when they arrived, and, in spite of professional medical skill, care and nursing, soon died. There were thirty-four left to be cared for. These were simply skin and bone when they first arrived. Some of them were covered with sores and vermin. All had an insatiable craving for food, which they could not digest. By incessant care, watching, nursing and medical treatment, they acquired health, gained flesh, and began to look like other healthy children.

"Their moral condition was worse than their physical degradation. Most of them came from a class of people called Bheels, in the Central Provinces, who are thieves by profession. This characteristic of the race was most prominent in these children. They were thievish, lying and deceitful in the extreme and showed little or no sense of moral responsibility.

"Special mention is due here to the share borne by Mrs. Chatterjee in the work of these schools; first in those for Hindu and Mohammedan girls, in which she was succeeded by her daughters, and second in the Girls' Orphanage and Boarding School. The latter was under her entire control from July, 1888, until early in 1916. To these schools and to the care of the women of the Christian families, this noble Christian lady devoted her life. One is tempted here to enlarge upon her share in all the activities of all those busy years. But she is, thank God, still with us, and we trust that she may live to bless others in the future as she has in the past. When that work shall have been completed, there will doubtless arise to tell of what her splendid unassuming life of service has meant to thousands. Meanwhile, we speak of her life and work only as inseparable from that of her beloved husband.

"The Denny Hospital for Women and Children was established in 1902, largely through the liberality of Miss Anna Denny of New York. Dr. Dora Chatterjee, on the completion of her course of Medical Training, in the U. S. A., was chosen as the head of this new institution, and continued in charge until her marriage, some eight years ago. Her work was greatly appreciated by the people and liberal grants were given to it by the Government."

To this outline of the more conspicuous and important of the opportunities of service, found and utilized, during his years of greatest activity, must be added mention of his ministration to the English Church of the Station. By invitation of the English residents, and with the sanction of the Bishop of the Diocese, in whom the control of the Church building was vested, he undertook the conduct of the Church service on every Sunday between the quarterly visits of the Chaplain of Jalandhar and continued to be responsible for this duty for more than forty years. We believe that this relation between the Indian minister and a British community is unique in the history of the Church of Christ in India. The minister was not only of a race other than the members of his congregation, but belonged to a branch of the Church other than that for whose use the building had been consecrated. The fruit of this special service was doubtless of immense value in its effect upon individual lives, and besides this, in binding the interest of the European people, most of them officials, to him and his work.

VII

HIS PLACE AS A LEADER IN THE CHURCH

Nothing is so misleading as to estimate the result of Indian Missions by the number of actual conversions.—*Prof. Satthianadhan.*

HAVING now sketched, in outline, the general course of his life, and indicated its main currents, and the beneficence of its influence within definite geographical limits, we come to speak of his usefulness in that sphere lying outside his immediate field of labor, wherein he came into touch with the Christian Church at large.

Within a very brief period after his settlement at Hoshyarpur, many unsought opportunities of coming into contact with the work of his own and other Missions, operating in the Panjab, began to offer themselves to him. In 1875 he was chosen by the Synod of India to a Lectureship in the Theological School at Allahabad, and occupied, for such time as he could be spared, that important position, until, indeed, the institution was closed, owing to the fact that the supply of students was largely exhausted, their services being immediately needed in the work of the several fields from which they had been sent.

In the Presbytery and Synod, he was a marked figure. His clearness of judgment, frankness of statement, and readiness to devote time and labor to the solution of difficulties, won for him such esteem in the Ecclesiastical Courts of his Church, that he was soon recognized as a leader. Many of us remember his long years of invaluable service as Stated Clerk of the Lahore Presbytery, during which, the promptness and accuracy with which he conducted all business coming before that body were most conspicuous. Similarly of the Synod of India, in the years preceding the formation of the Presbyterian Church in India, with its Synods and General Assembly, there were few, if any, individuals whose counsel was so eagerly sought or whose names were so inevitably to be found upon the more important committees.

One who now occupies a very exalted position in another branch of the Church, in speaking of a visit made by him to a meeting of the Synod of the Panjab, refers to a lengthy and somewhat tedious discussion as having been brought to a close by a few brief and final words from Dr. Chatterjee. This was a matter of frequent occurrence.

When, in 1884, the Theological Seminary was organized at Sahāranpur, he was one of the most active participants in the formation of plans for its efficient work, and sent from his district a large contingent of promising students.

Throughout all the years of the history of the institution, until his death, he served as a Director, and on several occasions, upon the invitation of the Faculty, delivered courses of lectures to the young men there undergoing courses of study in preparation for the Gospel ministry.

The Mission College at Lahore, in which Mr. Chatterjee, as we have seen, served for a time as a member of the staff, was compelled to discontinue its classes in 1869. In 1886, by action of the Mission, the College was re-opened with Rev. Dr. Forman as President and Rev. H. C. Velte, M.A., as Vice-President. This institution was placed under the immediate control of a Board of Directors. Of this Board, Dr. Chatterjee was chosen first

President, and continued uninterruptedly in that office for almost thirty years, or until October, 1915, when, owing to physical infirmity, he felt impelled to relinquish the active duties of this office and was made President *Emeritus*. An enthusiastic believer in Education as a missionary agency, he threw himself ardently into the task of helping to make the College a power in the Province. His wise counsel and hearty co-operation were, throughout all the years, from the days of small beginnings, to later times, when the college grew to a size and influence not anticipated by the founders, an asset of tremendous value. In recognition of his services, in this relation, a large addition to the buildings of the College made in 1910 was named the Chatterjee Science Block. In fulfilling the duties of his office, as President of the Board, his painstaking thoroughness was no less conspicuous than elsewhere. At the end of each year, he prepared and presented, through the Mission, to the Board in New York, a full and careful report of the working of the College Board and of the institution itself.

He early became intensely interested in all proposals looking toward the organic union of the several Presbyterian Churches in India, and one of the sore disappointments of his life was that he was not permitted to witness the union of all; though he never despaired of the eventual realization of his great desire.

Years before the formation of the Presbyterian Church in India, which involved, in his case and in the case of his Indian Brethren, and of the foreign members of the old Synod of India, separation from the Church in the United States, certain efforts looking toward the ultimate union of all Protestant Christians in the Panjab, had been initiated. With these most laudable efforts, the name of Rev. Robert Clark, M.A., of the Church Missionary Society, was conspicuously associated, and the movement was looked upon with favor by many others, including some members of the Panjab Mission. Dr. Chatterjee was deeply convinced of the importance of the Christian Church presenting an undivided front to the non-Christian world.

On one occasion, when delivering an address in America, at the ordination of the son of a beloved colleague, who was about to sail for India as a Missionary, he burst forth into such words as these: "I charge you, therefore, dearly beloved brother, not to allow the wildfire of sectarian partizanship to be carried along with you. Leave it in this land, or if one small spark of it should remain undētected, pray that it may be engulfed and extinguished in the bosom of the mighty ocean which you must cross before you reach the Indian shore."

He was eager that in his own life there should be nothing to separate him from the fullest sympathy and co-operation with Christians of all branches of the Church. He therefore entered heartily into certain tentative plans for co-operation, which it was hoped, by some, might lead to a closer federation, or even organic union, in coming years. These came largely to naught, through the unwillingness of some to concede enough to make even useful federation possible. He, along with many who agreed with him, would have rejoiced to find himself a member of a Church, whose Constitution would have included important elements of polity and practice absent from that of his own Church, provided that the new Church might have retained those features which he regarded as essential to the well being of the Body of Christ as a whole. Many of his warmest friends throughout life were from among the clergy and the laity of the Church of England and many of them contributed largely to the support of the work at Hoshyarpur. That he continued a Presbyterian was possibly a grief to some of them, but of this we are sure, that their love for him and their respect for his character could hardly, under any circumstances, have been greater than it was. All honor to them and to him, who were thus able to overlook denominational distinctions which they deplored but could not remove, and to unite in effort for the upbuilding of the Church.

In response to an invitation from the Bishop of Lahore, he with two other representatives of the Presbyterian Church, addressed the Anglican Diocesan Conference at Lahore in 1909, upon the topic of Church Union. In an address characterized by great breadth of charity and deep earnestness, he plead that an effort be made to close up the ranks of the Christian forces, in so far as Church government is concerned, and suggested that a modified episcopate might be adopted as a basis of union. The chief feature of the plan indicated was that men should be elected to the office of Bishop for a term of years, by clergy and laity, according to wisely formed and clearly defined rules. He contended that, if this concession were made to the non-Episcopal bodies, all remaining points of dif-

Mrs. Chatterjee in 1887
Picture taken in America

ference should be yielded by them in the interests of the great end sought to be attained. The discussion, on that occasion, was not wholly we may believe, unproductive of good, and yet neither speakers nor hearers were surprised that the particular suggestion failed to meet with any general acceptance. Reference to the address delivered by him at that time is, however, we think, justified because of the glimpse it affords us of his eagerness to see the people of the Lord become indeed one, and his readiness to join with his own Church, were the way to be made clear, in assuming a very large share in such concessions as must inevitably precede union. In a peculiar sense, he belonged to all the Churches. Ample testimony to this our readers will find both in the facts of his life and in the appreciations which will appear at a later point in this little volume.

While touching upon this matter of his loyalty to his own Church, and that breadth of sympathy which made it possible for him to work in harmony with people of various communions, it is fitting that we record some of the appreciations of the man and of his place in the Christian activities of his time furnished by those who recognized in this great Presbyterian a great Christian evangelist who belonged to the whole Church.

Here is a formal resolution passed by the Foreign Committee of that splendid society, which has stood in the very forefront of world-Evangelization during the whole of the period of what may be called modern Missions.

Church Missionary Society,
Salisbury Square, London, E. C.
July 18, 1916.

The Committee have received with regret the news of the death on May 31 of Dr. K. C. Chatterjee, late Moderator of the Presbyterian Church in India. They desire to express to that body and to Dr. Chatterjee's family their cordial sympathy in the loss sustained by the death of this beloved and eminent leader of the Indian Church and their admiration of and thankfulness to God for the work done and the witness borne by him. They recall with gratitude the help given by Dr. Chatterjee to many of their Missionaries in the work of Evangelization, his able co-operation in the work of the vernacular literature, and his ministrations in English under four Bishops in the Station Church at Hoshyarpur; and they pray that his life and example may prove to be the earnest of increasing leadership among Indian Christians.

(Signed) E. F. E. Wigram.
G. T. Manley.
Secretaries of the C. M. S.

A peculiarly discriminating estimate of the man has been furnished by one of the signatories to the above official document, who, for many years, a missionary in the Panjab, had the fullest opportunity of knowing the value to India and the Indian Church, of him of whom he writes. In a personal letter to the writer, the Rev. E. F. E. Wigram, M.A., Secretary of the Church Missionary Society, says:

> One thing that strikes me as I think over my own reminiscences of Dr. Chatterjee, is the strong firm lines of the impression produced by comparatively few strokes of contact with him. We did not come into very frequent intercourse, but none the less the impress left was a very clear and definite one. Outwardly there was that dignified and gracious presence, and it was the true expression of the man within. To be with him was to be braced and uplifted at once. His personality, without having a tinge of aggressive assertion in it, challenged you to be at your best, and yet more, to regard the best as the only possible. It was standing rebuke to anything petty or slipshod or unworthy in the servant of Christ.
>
> Then again he always gave the impression of a quiet reserve of strength sufficient for every emergency. He had his firm, strong grasp on the real essentials of the matter in hand; and he went forward as one confident as to the ultimate issue of the enterprise which engaged him, and

certain that he possessed the secret of the resources which would bring him victoriously through it. I have a particular recollection of the thrill with which I listened to probably the only sermon of his I have ever heard, preached to one of the earliest Panjab Student Conferences, held at Clarkabad, somewhere about 1899; and I am quite sure that it touched many of the hearts that heard it.

Lastly I cannot close without referring to Dr. Chatterjee's great contribution, alike conscious and unconscious, to the supreme cause of Unity. His unique relations to the first four Bishops of Lahore, while himself a member of the Presbyterian Church, are one signal illustration of this, and in point of fact we surely all claim him for our own, since he was manifestly Christ's. I have particularly happy recollections of a small Committee on Reunion, some years ago in which he took a leading and very encouraging part. He has gone now beyond the reach of dividing walls, and if anything can add to the unclouded vision of his Lord, I feel that it will be to witness his beloved India shake herself free from the trammels of our Western Divisions, and enter unitedly into the full heritage of the Catholic faith of Christ.

Another distinguished representative of the same society, who, for many years occupied a position of great and almost unique prominence in the Panjab, the Rev. H. U. Weitbrecht, D.D., has this to say of his association with Dr. Chatterjee and of the impression made by him upon men:

My first acquaintance with Dr. Chatterjee began in November, 1877, when the Rev. R. Bateman took me, then a budding missionary still in my first year, for an itineration, in company with Dr. Chatterjee, in the Hoshyarpur district. It was an invaluable experience to me in those early days and I was specially impressed with the work of the village of Ghorawaha, with its group of Christian families who had formerly been Mohammedan Rajputs. The impression then specially made upon me was, on the one hand, of the respect and reverence with which Dr. Chatterjee was regarded by his Christian fellow-workers, and his affectionate fatherly attitude towards them, and as regards outsiders, of his power of kindly and gentle persuasion together with shrewd reasoning which scarcely ever failed in quieting even bitter and abusive opponents. Later on I came in contact with Dr. Chatterjee chiefly in connection with the work of vernacular literature. He was an unfailing mainstay, especially of colportage work in connection with the Punjab Religious Book Society for many years. His annual reports always contained something of interest or suggestiveness and his counsel was never asked in vain. About the year 1902 we had a Conference for our colporteurs at St. John's Divinity School, in which he took part. Being in the hot weather we had to sleep side by side in the same room, for the sake of the punkah, and the impression then received of his devotional life remains with me. His friendship whenever we met or corresponded was a source of pleasure and of help both in human and divine life. Dr. Chatterjee's saintly yet strenuous life realized in a remarkable way the union of Christian grace and high-born Indian temperament. It will leave an indelible impression on generations to come.

No apology is surely needed for giving place here to still another estimate of the man, seen from the point of view of a countryman of his own, Principal S. K. Rudra, M.A., of the St. Stephen's College, Delhi, an institution in connection with the Cambridge Mission of the Church of England.

They, the Christians who came from the Scottish College in Calcutta, made the name of "Christian" a name respected in the Panjab. Dr. Kali Charan Chatterjee was pre-eminently one of these.

During my thirty years in the Panjab, I saw Dr. Chatterjee not more than six times. He seemed to live away from bustle and noise. I can vividly recall my first meeting. It was a pilgrimage. I came from Delhi to Jalandhar and rode nearly thirty miles in the only sort of rude conveyance I could get—the *Ekka*. It was nearly ten at night when I reached the house; and the first thing he asked me was if I was very tired by the ride. Everything was so new to me in the Panjab that I had not the slightest feeling of tiredness. I was struck by his question. But I know now as I know more of Ekkas also, that it was a fine feeling of sympathy which was the characteristic of a man, that prompted the question. The next morning

I saw him in his surroundings. An exceedingly plain house with plain furniture, plain food, severe almost in plainness, and himself, a tall, straight, lightly built man, but strong, with a fine impressive face, a noble brow, mobile lips, gentle but steady gaze, and a long flowing beard, clad in the good old Bengali style I knew, which gladdened my heart. He seemed thirty years behind the times. The quiet and simplicity of the man struck me greatly: there was no loudness of any sort. His voice and utterance, soft and thin, in measured and distinct words, counterparts of his physical aspect gave the key to his character. In the ordering of his home, it was just the same. No ostentation, no noise, no bustle, but it was all a deeply subdued, ordered life directed to the fulfilment of his vocation of being a Missionary to the Panjab peasants of Hoshyarpur. I was not disappointed in what I saw. I had never any occasion to revise this first impression of this servant of God. That was only strengthened as my acquaintance increased.

I must not attempt to chronicle my impressions of other meetings seriatim. It is sufficient to say that my first impressions were deepened and strengthened at every subsequent interview. I had seen him when all was well with him as the world goes, and I again saw him when he was laid low by domestic sorrows and bereavements. But he was ever the same in mind and demeanor, in faith and speech, only now riper in years, feebler in body, but not bent—straight and erect as ever, quiet and gentle, thinking of others; and by his life and conduct, bearing witness to the last that Christ alone is the Saviour of men.

He was present as a member in each of the Decennial Missionary Conferences, held in Calcutta in 1882, Bombay in 1892, and Madras in 1902. Both in the Bombay and Madras Conferences, he was a conspicuous figure. Before the former he read, by invitation of the Committee of Arrangements, a paper dealing with the subject of the Social and Legal Rights of Indian Christians, and spoke upon the subject of the Indian Church—the Training and Position of its Ministry. Remembering the circumstances which led to his leaving Calcutta, in his youth, and also the resolution at which he arrived, when he subsequently decided to devote his life to work in connection with a Missionary Society, we make no apology for reproducing here a few points from that address. Whatever variety of views may be held by good men and true, as to what principles should finally prevail as to the relation of our Indian brethren to the administration of funds, furnished by the Church in the West, few will be found to claim that the question has, as yet, been satisfactorily settled. It will be well worth while for those who are seeking after a better way than yet found, to heed the words of one so unquestionably unselfish, and earnestly desirous of the welfare of the Kingdom, as was our brother.

"The pay question ought not to be raised in a man's mind when he is entering into the ministry. He should not bargain for the Lord's service. The Missionary Societies may be relied upon to make provision for his necessary wants and comforts. If they do not, the Lord will. This has been my experience for thirty-two years. The question of position is a most vexatious question. Dr. Hooper avoids the discussion of it in his very thoughtful paper, and I do not wonder that he does so. I have seen it discussed for thirty-five years without producing any satisfactory result. It has no reference to the ecclesiastical positions of native ministers. This, as far as I know, is the same as that of Foreign Missionaries in all the Churches. It refers to their secular position in the management of mission affairs, and the administration of mission funds. All foreign missionaries, whether engaged in this country or sent out of Europe and America, enjoy this prerogative. All native ministers are denied it. There are two classes of native ministers. (*a*) Pastors. The connection of these is not with Mission Societies, but with churches to which they minister. (*b*) The second class is variously called evangelists, assistant missionaries and missionaries. The connection of these with Mission Societies is direct and permanent. They are agents of Mission Societies and not of the Indian Churches. They are their agents in the same sense that foreign missionaries are. My full conviction is, that those of them who are fitted by education and character to undertake the same duties and foreign missionaries ought to have the same position. Equal responsibilities imply equal power. Not to give them this power is to make an invidious distinction of race and color. Many reasons have been assigned for it, but none of them satisfactory. They are simply excuses. The present policy of Missionary Societies to native ministers of this class is a secular policy and based on worldly principles. It is a policy of injustice, suspicion and distrust, and cannot have the sanction and the blessing of the Master. Of course native ministers might give up the question of position and be content to serve the Lord in whatever position they are placed. Many of them are most cheerfully doing so. I am speaking of it on practical business principles.

These are strong words, and seem to indicate an uncompromising attitude on the part of the speaker. It is, however, to be remembered that he was assuredly not speaking on his own behalf. He had long years before decided the question for himself, and had resolved to desire nothing and ask nothing more than the privilege of spending his life in the relation to the Mission upon which he entered when he began the work in Hoshyarpur. He could have had a larger salary than the $36 a month allotted to him, and which sum remained constant throughout all the years of his ministry, but he never desired an increase. The Panjab Mission unanimously voted, on three occasions, to request the Board to appoint him a full member of the Mission, with voting power, and when it was discovered that this could not be, he uttered no word of disappointment or complaint. Few finer examples of Christian spirit have been seen in the modern Church.

VIII

HONORS AND APPRECIATIONS

A selfless man and stainless gentleman.—*Tennyson.*

IN the preceding pages an attempt has been made to present in very brief outline the course of this beautiful and devoted life as it touched and influenced great multitudes of India's people. The impression produced by his personality and work upon others, some of whom lived and worked in close relationship with him and some knew him but slightly, is of importance as we attempt to estimate the man and the special significance of his life.

Absorbed in the work of his station, singularly free from all desire for place or power among his brethren, nevertheless recognition of his character and influence was afforded by a variety of bodies and institutions.

In 1887, he with his wife and daughter Dora, visited the United States upon invitation of the Board of Foreign Missions. The visit was brief, extending over only five months, but the impression made by them was very great, first at the meeting of the General Assembly at Omaha, and subsequently in some of the important churches of the country. Upon this visit he was wont to look back with great pleasure, and it was during those brief months that not a few abiding friendships were formed with members of our Church in America.

In 1901 Government bestowed upon him the Kaisar-i-Hind Silver Medal in recognition of his public services to the City and District of Hoshyarpur. These services were conspicuous during a large portion of his life. Concerning them Mr. Wm. Coldstream, a prominent member of the Civil Service, has written:

"To outsiders, like myself, he seemed to occupy a unique and dominating position. No other missionary of Indian race in North India, so far as I know, has been brought by Providence into such a place. I had the privilege of his intimate friendship for forty years, and have seen and admired the growing usefulness of his career.

"To the primary qualifications for his life's work, he added a persuasive force of character and a capacity for affairs, which made him most useful in spheres outside the direct duties of his calling. In common with other District officers of Hoshyarpur, I had a great reliance on the soundness of his advice and the wisdom of his counsel. The public of Hoshyarpur owed him much, for he was a prominent and public-spirited citizen. He was a member of the Municipal Board, and I recall the sane and helpful position he took in delicate and difficult matters.

"In beginning his work, in the early sixties, in Hoshyarpur, Dr. Chatterjee was happy in having Mr. Henry Perkins as head of the District, for that critical time, he was sure of sympathy and also of support, so far as it was possible for a Government official to give it. But Dr. Chatterjee was never dependent upon, nor even sought for, the favor of the authorities, as such, in the promotion of his work.

"His works do follow him. He will always be remembered as the founder of the Hoshyarpur Mission, and its strength for more than half a century. His work was in the foundations, at a time when building was slow and difficult. The edifice will remain for all time to the Glory of God, and the benefit of the country of his adoption, where he filled such an honored place and was so blessed to the upbuilding of a strong Christian Church."

He interested himself in the life of the people and was in himself an illustration of the possibility and desirability of presenting the beauty and power of Christianity in ways other than that of direct preaching, without in any degree losing sight of such preaching as the central purpose of his life.

Another prominent civilian, Col. Gordon Young, has written of Dr. Chatterjee, and his great power in Hoshyarpur as follows:

"Very soon after my arrival, Mr. Chatterjee paid me a visit, and I found him to be of singularly engaging and pleasing manners and address, and we soon became very friendly. In the hot season, when dressed completely in white, he would stand leaning on his long bamboo alpenstock—what with his flowing beard, his turbanned head and his benevolent expression, he presented a truly apostolic figure.

"We all recognized in Mr. Chatterjee a man of highest Christian character, full of grace and of good works—of the sweetest temper, and the friend of all the natives of the District, whether they received him as a spiritual leader and teacher or not. I received ample testimony to this very soon by both Hindus and Mohammedans.

"Naturally, as a Christian missionary who constantly preached in a Bazaar, he had religious disputations with men of all religious beliefs, but however much they disagreed with his doctrine, all respected, and many loved him. His influence always made for peace.

"I recall especially the case of 'Ghorawaha,' where Mr. Chatterjee's good temper and wisdom were conspicuous, in a matter which at one time looked serious. Amongst the Christian converts in the village mentioned were several Mohammedan Rajputs—a proud and independent class of Zemindars and a certain Moulvi, himself bitterly opposed to Christianity, made an attempt to deny these men access to their own drinking wells, asserting that the vessels they used would defile the water. This naturally gave rise to much ill feeling, and the idea spread quickly and was adopted in other towns and villages in the District. It became necessary, therefore, to institute proceedings in the Criminal Courts against the Moulvi and his faction, as a serious breach of the peace seemed likely to occur. The Christians, of course, had to give evidence, and their pastor amongst them—though much against his will.

"Efforts were made by some of the most loyal native gentlemen to compose the dispute, but the case had been instituted by order of the Government, and it was not possible to give away the missionaries' cause and yield to the noisy Mohammedan faction—till Mr. Chatterjee himself, came forward, and begging that the prosecution might be abandoned in the interest of peace, managed to secure full recognition of the Christion converts at the hands of their opponents.

"Mr. Chatterjee was, without any exception, the most successful missionary I ever met. He had a little circle of Christians when I first knew him, consisting of his own household, a Catechist or two, and perhaps one or two converts only, but in the course of four or five years, these had expanded to some scores, and there are now, I believe, between five or six thousand; all the work of one servant of God."

It remains to quote from still another of the "Rulers of the Panjab." Sir Wm. Mackworth Young, Lieutenant Governor of the Province from 1897-1902, has sent this striking estimate of our departed brother:

"I had the privilege of Dr. Chatterjee's friendship from March, 1869, when I was stationed at Hoshyarpur through October, 1870. The beloved

Henry Perkins was Deputy Commissioner, so the Civil Station and the Missionary Quarters were in complete harmony. Chatterjee, in the absence of a Government Chaplain, used to hold a Sunday Service for the Station, and greatly did we value his ministrations. His sermons were always most instructive, and he was a close student of the best books, Alfred's Greek Testament being one of his favorites. This happy relation between him and the English residents of the Station continued for many years. No less than five Bishops cordially approving of his gratuitous ministrations. We became fast friends, and remained such after we ceased to be near neighbors. He was one of the most attractive men I ever met. With great gentleness and selflessness he combined a clear judgment and a firm purpose. I remember his dining with me in camp, and refusing meat. Asked the reason, he said he had given it up because a young enquirer had turned his back upon him, when he had seemed to be attracted by his preaching, because he saw a fowl hanging up in his kitchen 'shuldari' ready to be cooked for his dinner. He acquired great influence in the neighborhood owing to his sympathy and reasonableness, and was on several occasions useful in local disputes. For many years he discharged public duties to which he was appointed by election or by order of the Government, and exhibited the qualities which, when fully developed, led to his becoming Moderator of the General Assembly of the Presbyterian Church in India. He always seemed to me to be the most perfect embodiment of Oriental Christianity known to me during my Indian experience."

The above will suffice to show what an extraordinary degree he was able to bring the impress of his Christian personality to bear upon all classes of the community. These testimonies, selected from amongst many, and because of lack of space greatly abbreviated, will it is hoped, enable those who read this record to recognize something of the possibilities in the life of a Missionary in India, in its influence upon a great community and the impress it may have upon those who are placed as rulers in the land. And here it is fitting that mention be made of the debt owed by the Church at large to a group of English civilians in the Panjab whose influence as Christian men has, ever since the annexation in 1849, been a mighty factor in the establishment of the Kingdom. They were not free to teach or to preach Christianity, but their lives, their sympathy and their prayers have left behind them an impress that can hardly be overestimated. There have been such men as Lord Lawrence and his brother Henry, Sir Herbert Edwardes, Sir Donald McLeod, Sir Charles Aitchison, Sir Robert Montgomery and others including those whose words have been quoted above.

In 1901, the Degree of Doctor of Divinity

was conferred upon Mr. Chatterjee by Washington and Jefferson College. Nine years later the same honorary Degree was conferred upon him, side by side with the Lord Bishop of Canterbury and our own Mr. Robert E. Speer, by the Chancellor of the University of Edinburgh.

In speaking of honors received, he said:

"I never sought any of them. I could have been quite happy and content with the honor of being a servant of Jesus Christ and a laborer in His vineyard. They came to me as the gifts of God, intended for His glory and I accepted them gratefully. 'It is my Father that honoreth me.'"

In 1910 he attended as a delegate of the Presbyterian Church the great Edinburgh Conference.

Mr. Gairdner in his account of that great assemblage, speaks of Dr. Chatterjee in these graphic words:

"Among the members of the Conference is yonder venerable—one might say high-priestly—figure. A pure Brahman by descent, with long silky-white beard, tall-uprightly figure, aristocratic gentle features, and mild Indian voice; a Bengali convert of the great Dr. Duff; now an honored minister of the Panjab, chosen to be the first Moderator of the Presbyterian Church in India."

It is also recorded that on one of the days of the great Conference which was attended by twelve hundred delegates from all parts of the world and leaders of the most important sections of the Christian Church and the Missionary Societies and Boards, the morning worship in the great Assembly Hall in Edinburgh was led by Dr. Chatterjee, "The venerable delegate from India."

The years following that memorable visit in 1910, witnessed a gradual weakening of his bodily powers. The people of India do not, as a rule, retain their full physical and mental powers to so great an age as do those whose lives are spent in the West. And yet up to within a few months of his departure from us, at the ripe age of seventy-seven years, Dr. Chatterjee continued to labor with great efficiency, guiding with remarkable wisdom the affairs of his great field.

Meanwhile he welcomed to a share in the duties and responsibilities connected with City and District, first, two lady missionaries, Miss Margaret Given and Miss Caroline Downs, the latter of whom after a life of long and beautiful service, passed to her reward in 1914; and later the Rev. A. B. Gould and his wife Mrs. Helen Newton Gould, also Miss A. M. Kerr.

For several years, having become conscious of his failing powers, he faced the inevitable day, when he should be compelled to retire from active participation in the things that had claimed the many years of his vigorous manhood. Opportunities for counsel with those whom he recognized as his closest friends were eagerly sought, and his scrupulous anxiety lest he might, by continuing in it too long, injure the work into which he had poured the energies of a lifetime, was obvious to all.

Those who were present at the annual meeting of the Directors of the Forman Christian College in 1914, will never lose from memory the impression made upon them by the words spoken when he rose at the close of the first session, to ask permission to retire from the presidency of that body, an office which he held uninterruptedly for a period of twenty-eight years. Moved by deep emotion, so great as to, in some measure, hinder the fullest utterance, he told us of his love for the College, his estimate of the great work it had done and would still do, and referred to this necessity for breaking the ties which had been growing stronger and stronger during all the years, and this stepping aside into a life of comparative inactivity as the greatest trial of his life.

A few days later, at the meeting of the Panjab Mission, he expressed his desire to be relieved of a large part of his work, and in accordance with his wish, the work of the District with its great body of Christians dwelling in the villages, was transferred to the charge of Mr. and Mrs. Gould. Another year of gradually increasing weakness followed, yet it was by no means a year of inactivity, but one of real helpfulness and power amongst the comparatively few people whom he was still able to touch by the influence of his life and counsel. The members of his family and all those who knew him best shrank from the crisis which was sure to come when the last of the ties which bound him to his beloved Hoshyarpur should be severed. When the members of the Mission were assembled in October, 1915, he was with them, but unable to attend many of the sessions. Feeling that he could not bear the strain of addressing them from the floor of the house, he penned and sent in to be read a remarkable letter, full of expression of that love which he felt for them all, and of appreciation of the confidence which had been reposed in him, and of his gratitude to God for the privilege of serving together with them for so many years in relations of courtesy, confidence and mutual affection.

Compelled to share his conviction that he should be set free from all work and responsibility and in the earnest hope that he and his wife might be spared for future years of less strenuous service, than would be required of them were they to remain in their old station, the members of the Mission unanimously took such action as provided for their comfortable residence at Phillour in the immediate neighborhood of the Rev. H. Golaknath, a brother of Mrs. Chatterjee. After this removal, Dr. Chatterjee left his new home on but one occasion, and that was when he attended a meeting of the Presbytery at Jalandhar. His ability to endure the fatigue of even so short a journey was questioned, and yet he felt that he must attend that meeting in order that he might personally arrange the final disposition of some items of business in connection with which he had not up to that time been able to divest himself of all responsibility.

He returned home in a condition of great weakness, which continued until May 31st, 1916, when he entered into rest.

On the evening of the day following we laid his body to rest in the little cemetery at

Hoshyarpur. A great multitude gathered to do honor to his memory. There were the members of his family, many members of the Panjab Mission, scores of Indian Christian men and women, who knew him as their spiritual father, and felt that the world would be very empty for them without him, Hindus, Mohammedans and Sikhs, to the number of many hundreds, and the European officials of the Station.

As, the service over, we turned from the place, one thought concerning the preëminently useful life that had closed was paramount. The conviction was borne in upon the mind that the real secret of the unfailing power and beauty of the service that had so blessed Hoshyarpur, and reached far beyond into the greater world could be found in the experience of that morning many years ago, when husband and wife with one mind and heart had turned from the temptation to enter a walk of life where more of wealth and fame were promised them, and had deliberately chosen to spend their days, as they believed, in obscurity, themselves unrecognized by the world, that they might with all their powers, serve Him whom they loved, and whose voice they were convinced that they had heard.

IX

THE MAN AS SEEN BY HIS COLLEAGUES

"The fragrance of the knowledge of Christ."

UPON hearing of his call to rest, the Board of Foreign Missions of the Presbyterian Church in the U. S. A., under whose auspices he had labored for so long, passed the following minute:

"With the feeling of special grief and personal loss, the Board received tidings by mail from the Panjab Mission of the death on the evening of May 31st, 1916, of the Rev. K. C. Chatterjee of Hoshyarpur.

"Dr. Chatterjee was a unique figure in the councils and work of the Christian Church in India. His parents were high caste Hindus, and as a Brahman youth he entered Dr. Duff's college in Calcutta, and through Dr. Duff's influence was led at the age of twenty to become a Christian. Upon graduation he became the headmaster of the Jullundar Mission School, and later Professor of Mathematics in one of the colleges in Lahore. In 1868 he was ordained and took charge of the work in the Hoshyarpur district, where for many years he has been pastor of one of the largest native Churches in India, besides having care of all the missionary work throughout the district. In 1887 he visited the United States, where he was greatly honored among the Churches, and left behind him when he returned to India the fragrance of his high devotion and noble character. For over twenty-five years he has been president of the Board of Directors of Forman College. In 1903 he was made Moderator of the First General Assembly of the Presbyterian Church in India. He was one of the representatives of the Presbyterian Board of Foreign Missions at the World Missionary Conference in Edinburgh in 1910, where he received the degree of Doctor of Divinity from Edinburgh University. Dr. Chatterjee was honored and beloved by all the missionaries as one of their wisest leaders and truest friends, and he was respected and revered by all classes of the population, Brahmans and low castes, Europeans, Eurasians and Indian Christians.

"Mrs. Chatterjee, who survives her husband, was a daughter of the Rev. Golak Nath, the first Brahman convert in our Presbyterian Missions. One of Dr. Chatterjee's daughters took a medical course in the United States and until her marriage worked with her parents in Hoshyarpur. His other children have all honored their parentage. The Board extends to them and to the Missions and to the Church in India its deep sympathy in this great loss, and records its gratitude to God for the noble character and far-reaching influence of one who gave himself wholly to Jesus Christ as his Lord and served Him with signal ability through a long and blameless life."

The Opening of the "K. C. Chatterjee Science Building" of the Forman Christian College. Messrs. Chatterjee, Wherry, Velte and Orbison Seated; the President Speaking.

The relationship existing between members of the same Mission in a Foreign land is frequently very close and tender. Owing, however, to inherent diversities in temperament and the presence of "human nature" even in very devoted Christians, cases of serious differences of opinion out of which more or less grave misunderstandings have arisen, are not unheard of. But it is only just to say that these are comparatively rare, surprisingly so when one bears in mind the circumstances in which they live and labor. Though not technically a "full" member of the Panjab Mission, he and his devoted and charming wife were given a place in the confidence, intimate friendship and affection of the members of that body second to none. Many of Dr. Chatterjee's most intimate friends and associates had preceded him to the heavenly rest. Notable among these because of their relation to him in the earlier days of his ministry, were Rev. John Newton, and Rev. Chas. W. Forman, D.D., but one thinks of a score or more of others, who, were they here to speak, could tell of days and years of precious fellowship with this prince amongst men, who counted it all joy to serve with them the Master whom they all loved. Amongst those who remain a few preëminently qualified through long association and personal friendship, to estimate the man and his work, have responded to a request for some such statement.

The Rev. E. M. Wherry, D.D., of Ludhiana writes:

The trait in his character which most impressed me was his love. He was uniformly gentle in his treatment of others. Under provocation he was very self-possessed. I never saw him resent an injury. He would smile and even seek to condone the injury. His thoughtful interest in the poor Christians of his district was most marked. Where pecuniary aid would be an injurious precedent, he would plan relief in some way consistent with the charity. In ecclesiastical meetings and in conferences, where he was strenuously engaged, his manner was uniformly respectful and courteous. His counsel was marked by wisdom. He always had a wide perspective and foresaw the ultimate effect of legislation. Among our Indian brethren no one did more to promote the union of the various Presbyterian bodies to constitute a National Presbyterian Church. We all recognized this fact and voiced our belief in making him the first Moderator.

In all his work he had the aid and counsel of his wife, who shared in all his anxieties and aided in all his work. As a consultative member of our Mission, as Moderator, in Presbytery and as a delegate to General Assembly, he never failed to do the Master's will.

The Rev. J. J. Lucas, D.D., of Allahabad, writes:

In 1884 Dr. Chatterjee was elected Moderator of the Synod of North India, the first Indian called to that position; the Missionary who presented his name with a few words of appreciation, was asked as he left the Ludhiana Church that morning, whether it was proper to speak of a man in his presence and at once it was brought to his memory how often Paul praised his fellow-workers, and that in open letters to be read by them and by the whole Church. He might have added that such words of appreciation would rather deepen the sense of demerit in men like Dr. Chatterjee, rather than fill them with pride. And so it was, for in all the years that followed bringing honor after honor to our beloved Dr. Chatterjee, they left him the same humble, gracious, gentle, loving disciple of the Lord Jesus. There was something in his presence and speech and life that the apostle calls "The fragrance of the knowledge of Christ"—that something which like a fragrance is so pervasive and so indefinable, but which is felt, and which, after all, is the best witness to the life of the Lord Jesus in the heart. When elected by a unanimous vote Moderator of the first General Assembly of the Presbyterian Church in India, he was deeply moved and spoke of many influences which had wrought together in the hand of God to mould and shape his life. When a year later he opened the Assembly with a sermon, he revealed the secret of his life in the message he gave to his fellow-workers—"Even the youths shall faint and be weary, and the young men shall utterly fall, but they that wait on the Lord shall renew their strength; they shall mount up with wings as eagles; they shall run and not be weary; they shall walk and not be faint." Herein is the secret of the strength and beauty of Dr. Chatterjee's life; its humility and dignity, its fragrance and fruitfulness, its unweariedness in the service of Christ, and its patient continuance in well-doing unto the very end.

The Rev. E. P. Newton of Khanna, writes:

I have known Dr. Chatterjee for 42 years, and have met him and been brought into close relations with him many times during that period.

Among the points in his character which impressed me was entire trustworthiness. During practically that whole time he was in whole charge of the work in the Hoshyarpur district, and he set an example to all of us of faithfulness and diligence in the discharge of his duties. It was only when increasing age and ill health began to weigh heavily on him that the growth and remarkable prosperity of the work led him to ask for the help of a colleague.

He was also a hard worker. Apart from the care of a large Christian community in the city and district, he was always engaged in literary work directed to the furtherance of the gospel and the upbuilding of the Church in this country. He was a faithful preacher in city and village, and with Mrs. Chatterjee conducted a boarding school for Christian girls in Hoshyarpur.

Dr. Chatterjee was a humble minded minister of Christ. He was a Brahman of high educated attainments, yet devoted his life chiefly to evangelistic and pastoral work among the outcaste population of his district, and his self-denying efforts were in an eminent degree fruitful. Indeed at a time when in all other districts of our Mission there were, in the villages, no Christians, he had already gathered large numbers into the Church. Never once have I heard him call attention to his high caste origin. To him all Christians were his brothers in Christ, and all others, whether high or low in the world's estimation, were equally in need of the regenerating grace of God, and the atoning blood of Christ, in which alone he himself trusted. When he turned his back on Hinduism, and in baptism confessed the faith of Christ, he unreservedly threw in his lot with Christ's people and accepted the Gospel as the sole rule of his life. Though his home was in Bengal, and he was by nationality a Bengali, yet almost the whole of his life was spent in the Panjab. Here he lived, worked, and died, loved and respected by all who knew him, both European and Indian, and his death has left a gap in the Indian Church of this province which it will be hard to fill.

The Rev. H. C. Velte of Saharanpur, writes:

It is not easy to write down one's impressions of Dr. Chatterjee for all one can say seems so inadequate, falls short of what he really was. His greatness consisted not so much in any one preëminent virtue, as in a combination of all those qualities that constitute the ideal Christian character, or make the perfect man in Christ. Perhaps it may be also said that it was in the passive rather than in the active virtues of the

Christian life that Dr. Chatterjee excelled. He reminded one of St. John rather than of St. Paul. The graces which made his life so beautiful and so lovely, were the graces St. Paul enumerates as the fruit of the Spirit: love, joy, peace, long-suffering, kindness, goodness, faithfulness, meekness, self-control. Dr. Chatterjee's nobleness was of the highest kind, not nobleness of birth, though he possessed that too, but nobleness of character, and of a character in which all the virtues of a Christian life were blended together into one harmonic whole.

Perhaps if we begin to analyze Dr. Chatterjee's character, we shall find that the outstanding quality in it was his devotion to the Lord Jesus Christ. Almost the last words that fell from his lips were these, "I am the servant of the Lord Jesus Christ." With Zinzendorf he might have said, "I have but one passion, and that is Jesus." From the time of his conversion to his last day he truly and whole-heartedly loved and served the Saviour, to whom he owed so much, and his love to Christ burned with more and more brightness to the end.

Among the qualities that impressed me, and I am sure many others who knew him, was the simplicity of his faith. "In all the best men you meet," someone has said, "the thing that is most peculiar about them is the child's heart they bear within the man's." Dr. Chatterjee was a man of great faith, but what made it so great was that he ever carried with him the spirit of a little child. In his conversations, in his sermons, but above all in his prayers, did his simple childlike faith reveal itself.

Another feature that made him so lovable to all was his gentleness and courtesy. In him the

Christian gentleman was seen almost to perfection. It is impossible to associate him with anything unseemly or unfitting. He frequently was a guest at our house, and we always felt that his very presence was a benediction. And all this courtesy came to him so naturally.

Modesty and humility were also very striking features in Dr. Chatterjee's character. Though like Paul he might have had confidence in the "flesh" and indulged in boasting, but he never did; he was free from all pride. He was only a poor sinner whom Jesus had saved. Though born of the highest of Brahman families, yet he mingled freely with his poor low caste brethren; in fact he was one of the first in the Punjab Mission to begin work among these classes, bringing thousands of them to Christ. And in his intercourse with all classes there was the same modesty and humility.

Conscientiousness and faithfulness were also striking qualities in Dr. Chatterjee's character. He had a very high sense of duty. He was ever conscious of his responsibility not to men but to his Divine Master, and his aim was to be well pleasing to Him. His accounts were always in perfect order. Every letter he received was promptly and carefully answered. Every duty assigned to him was most faithfully performed. His reports to Committees and to the Mission were never a day late. Character often reveals itself in little things and it was in the little things that Dr. Chatterjee proved himself so faithful, and therein we see the greatness of the man.

In the light of these appreciations of Dr. Chatterjee and his work, there seems little need that more be said concerning the significance of his life. In his personality, in his many-sided capacity he was an unusual man. He doubtless would have done good work in a field other than India, and have risen to a position of more or less prominence amongst his fellows.

In the relationship of intimate friendship, for more than a quarter of a century, he revealed himself in such a way as to make it easy for one to recognize and approve the fidelity of the pictures drawn by those whose words have been quoted.

In estimating the significance of his life, it is well to consider the bearing of such a career upon the whole question of effort on behalf of the class which, in his youth, he represented.

The slow progress of the Gospel amongst the higher castes and more or less enlightened peoples of India is well known and greatly lamented. Some of the causes of this have been alluded to elsewhere, but a full discussion of them would be clearly beyond the limits which we have set for this sketch.

But that the efforts of Christian Missions amongst the educated classes have resulted in failure is very far from being true. When Kali Charan Chatterjee was converted through the agency of a Christian School and College, through his conversion that school set in motion a long line of influences that eventually touched the lives of many thousands. A great force came into operation when he forsook the faith of his fathers.

In spite of the very valid objections to comparisons which we all recognize, the statement is here ventured that to the writer, at least, no missionary in India of any race or country, has been known regarding whom it could be affirmed, with any degree of confidence that the fruit of his life was more rich than that borne by the life of our departed brother.

The fact that a knowledge of the Gospel of Jesus Christ wrought this marvelous transformation in a life that had its beginnings in a form of teaching and in practices so absolutely at variance with the teachings and the life of Jesus constitutes an abiding ground of confidence for the future. It is worth remembering that the power that came to him lifted him from out the Pantheism and Polytheism with which his mind and heart had in childhood been impregnated and saturated, into the acceptance, in the most whole-hearted manner, of the entire substance of Christian revelation, and that this work had been accomplished by the time he had reached the years of full manhood. Thus there lay before him on the day of his baptism a life of full three-score years, and we have seen how he used them.

Scores of others, born and reared under similar conditions, there have been whose lives and labors have illustrated the same things, and teach us not only that there is no occasion for despondency, but also that in labor for the class which embraces the natural leaders of the masses of the people, the Church has before her a sphere of unlimited opportunity and promise.

Individuals from amongst this portion of the population are responding to the message of Christ, here one and there another, and these are enriching the Church in her leadership, a leadership possessed of a quality which would have been largely lacking, had it not been for the form of work which the uninformed have sometimes characterized as a failure. Many of these are, with enthusiasm and power like to that shown by the Chatterjees, throwing themselves into effort for the lowly, the ignorant, the "untouchable," who today are responding in thousands to the invitation of the Gospel.

The brother who has gone has left to his Indian brethren a message of hope. Where he walked they too may walk and win the same victory. A lamentable thing it will be if the young men of India fail to catch the stimulus of his life.

It is to be regretted that more of the people of the West did not have an opportunity of seeing and knowing him. Had this been possible, they would unquestionably have found through their knowledge of him, not only occasion to thank God for what He wrought through one who came out from Brahmanism unto Christ, but would also have seen in him and in the great company represented by him, though still unwilling to accept Christ, that which would have finally convinced them that there is no more urgent and promising field for Christian effort to be found anywhere than that furnished by the people from amongst whom Kali Charan came.

One of the great sons of that land, who himself, alas! never touched but the hem of the Saviour's garment, but who nevertheless seemed to have caught some vision of the things that are to be, once said:

"None but Jesus, none but Jesus deserves to wear the bright and glorious diadem of India,—and Jesus shall have it."

Shall we Christians say less than this?

X

THE OLD AND THE NEW

IT is still, in spite of all the changes that have taken place in the attitude of many, indeed an appalling prospect that is faced by a Hindu when he stands on the brink of decision for Christ. He must literally forsake all if he would follow Jesus. This he knows in a general way, but only realizes in its fullest meaning in the days that follow the public profession of his faith. He has to fight his way through a host of antagonisms and obstructions, sufficient to appal, if not to overpower, a man of ordinary courage and determination.

Young converts have been kidnapped, imprisoned, tortured, even put to death. Some have disappeared never to be heard of more. The intensity of caste and racial feeling and the cruel bigotry manifested in connection with it cannot be readily imagined by those who have not come into direct contact with it. A Brahman, well known to me, was a drunkard and a notorious profligate. He heard the message of the Gospel, and having accepted it was baptized. His faithful wife hearing of this fled from their home in horror. A drunken and unclean husband she could endure, but not a Christian, a man who had violated the rules of caste. Scores of times we have heard from the lips of earnest seekers after God, such cries as these: "I cannot break my mother's heart." "Such disgrace will surely kill my father." "I will be a Christian at heart, but cannot bring sorrow and shame upon those whom I love, by breaking caste." Are we greatly surprised that all hesitate and many turn away altogether in face of these tremendous difficulties? We are told, and with truth, that the power of caste is decreasing, but any marked change in this particular is largely confined to the dwellers in the cities and larger towns. In the little hamlets of the land where are found the majority of the total population, little alteration in the attitude of the people toward their own or others' caste privileges and obligations is to be discerned. It is further to be noted that even where rules have been relaxed and many of the more enlightened have come to the point of openly disregarding the observances enjoined by the Shastras and enforced by custom, another force has entered to preserve the family and caste from disintegration. This may be described as a certain family or racial pride. In every large and enlightened community men who themselves disregard every rule of caste, are unremitting in their watchfulness against any defection from that which they desire to be maintained as a national faith. These stand ready to employ measures no less drastic than those employed by the rigidly orthodox, in order to combat any tendency upon the part of the individual or the family to identify themselves with the faith of Christ.

In the case of Kali Charan and others of that period, the opposition from which they suffered was due perhaps almost exclusively to the strong conviction based upon religious sentiment that to abandon the principles and observances of the ancestral faith meant utter disaster to the individual for time and eternity. When it is remembered that the orthodox Hindu finds it impossible to even think of life as a thing apart from religion, and that every important circumstance of his sojourn here has to him a profound religious significance, we begin to understand something of the nature of the shock with which even the suggestion of a change in faith comes to one whose whole being is impregnated with this idea as to the scope and content of religion in relation to his personality. It may be said that he is born, eats, sleeps, bathes, marries, and dies religiously, or, in any case, ceremonially; and a definite breaking away from this ceremonial religion is a cutting loose not merely from an unimportant feature of his being, but from absolutely every thing that he has been taught to value. Although, as has been said, Dr. Chatterjee was not wont to dwell upon the things that he suffered, we have no reason to doubt that his experiences were in no way less trying than those through which we have seen others pass. As we contemplate the young lad stepping forth from his home in obedience to the call of God we see the beginnings of that triumph of faith which was so wonderfully beautiful and so permanently obvious up to the last hour of his earthly service.

It was no mere intellectual process through which he passed. That might conceivably have accounted for the earliest steps in his career; indeed, instances are by no means lacking to prove that mental conviction has sometimes sufficed to carry the convert up to and even beyond the stage of public profession of faith through baptism. That God wrought a work of grace in his heart cannot be doubted. Quietly, unflinchingly, he made a public declaration, and then, as the years passed, he continued to grow in Christian knowledge and power, thus being prepared for the work of eminent usefulness to which in the maturity of his powers he was called. Nothing could have been more whole hearted than his renunciation of both Hindu doctrine and ceremonial. Many will recall the fervor with which he led the old Synod of India in a protest against the introduction, or the use of individual cups at Communion. All could not follow his argument or share his disapproval; but to him the innovation seemed to mean but one thing, the encouragement of caste feeling in the Church, and he would have none of it.

In his youth the enquiring spirit had before it fewer alternatives than now. Then the choice was, in general, between philosophic Hinduism with all its implications on the one hand, and on the other, either acceptance of the fundamental doctrines of Christianity, or the entire rejection of the supernatural. And yet, there were not a few who shrank from accepting any one of these positions. So long ago as 1828, or a full decade before the birth of Kali Charan, Rammohan Roy had laid the foundations of the Brahmo Somaj; but from the time of his death in 1833 until 1841 it had gained but little influence. During the period, therefore, when the many converts to Christianity were gathering about the Scottish Missionaries in Calcutta, it is to be remembered that before them there were but three alternatives: Old Hinduism, Christianity or Atheism. As the years passed, many "half-way houses" between the older faith of their fathers and the full acceptance of Christ were established. The Brahmo Somaj under the leadership of such men as Devendra Nath Tagore and Keshab Chandra Sen, offered to the young Hindu a monotheistic faith, which, however, repudiated or ignored the Christian idea of the Deity of Jesus Christ. Later in 1875, the Arya Somaj came into being with its doctrine of the unity of God and the absolute and exclusive authority of the Vedas. These organizations, not to speak of a score or more of minor ones, have continued during the years that have elapsed since their origin, to invite into their membership the man who.

revolting against idolatry, and the grosser evils of his ancestral faith, still not unnaturally shrinks from an open and complete rupture with Hinduism. This is in itself sufficient to account for the fact that in more recent years comparatively few college students have been found to pass at one step from the older form of faith into the full acceptance of Jesus Christ as Saviour and Lord.

Dr. Chatterjee loved to dwell, in later years, upon the marvelous changes witnessed by him in India during his lifetime. His life covered indeed a period more remarkable than any previous one in the history of the country, for the transformations it witnessed. A great intellectual awakening began in the early days of the nineteenth century, and the first modern religious movement, as has been seen, only a quarter of a century later. This is not the place in which to analyze the forces which co-operated to produce this particular awakening; but it may safely be affirmed that there were, in general, two, namely, the operations of the British Government and the activities of the Protestant Missionary Societies. Government on the one hand entered upon a programme of reform, condemning and prohibiting customs that were immoral and revolting, in spite of the sacredness which was supposed to attach to many of them. On the other hand the Missionary, the real ally of the Government, though not in the outset recognized as such, was busy not only with the primary task of preaching the Gospel but with the work of furthering every cause that had as its object the social and domestic uplift of the people.

New ideals fired the imagination of hundreds even in the early days of the last century. The way was rapidly prepared for numberless social reforms; and movements which had their origin then have so grown in form and in the extent of their influence that the minds and lives of many millions of men and women have been touched and elevated by them. The India of today is not the India of three-quarters of a century ago. It may be doubted indeed whether any country has undergone greater changes in life and thought during such a period, than those which mark the history of Hindustan during that time.

Old India is, however, still recognizable. A land which produced the Vedas, the two great Epic poems, and the six systems of Philosophy and found expression for its life and thought in these, is not readily transformed into something new. A great Mohammedan population of sixty-six millions which began its growth more than eight centuries ago, does not abandon its creed in a day. But the conviction that the great work to be done in India can only be said to have been well begun, does not lessen one's feeling of amazement as he compares the conditions of today with those of the days preceding the great upturning of 1857. One of the new conditions is well illustrated in the Hoshyarpur District itself. When the Mission was first opened, accessions to the Church were exceedingly few. No single community was as a whole inclined to give the Missionary a hearing. A movement began among the *chuhras* in 1888, and out from amongst the approximately twenty thousand persons belonging to that class large numbers have been enrolled as members of the Church. Throughout that entire region of the Panjab, the Mass movement still grows in volume, and people are literally pressing into the Church. Evangelists and pastors are face to face with a tremendous problem, or rather a series of problems. They dare not admit to the Communion of the Church those who have not been in some measure instructed; and yet the task of providing adequate means of instruction is appallingly great.

At the beginning of the period of which we speak, the years covered by the active life of our great evangelist, the Church in India was both small and weak. He lived to see a large growth in both numbers and spirituality. He saw its membership in the beginnings of what we believe to be an era of self-propagation, self-government and self-support. Although the numerical results of village work in his hands and in the hands of his brethren, were so great in comparison with those resulting from the employment of School and College as evangelizing agencies, he never faltered in his belief that the latter should be maintained in fullest operation, not only for the sake of the Christian Community, but as practically the only available method of evangelizing the classes lying outside the scope of the Mass movement. It is remembered how on one occasion he pointed with satisfaction to the Missionaries of the National Missionary Society laboring in the Panjab, and to the membership of the Panjab Committee of Management, as "almost without exception students of our College."

He was a conservative in Theology. In the

days of his preparation for licensure he carefully studied the works of Dr. Chas. Hodge of Princeton, and accepted fully the system of Theology which he found there. When once his own early doubts had been removed, before his baptism, his faith in the Divine Word as the ultimate authority in all matters of belief and practice was apparently immovable. He seemed to regard with a feeling akin to amazement the state of doubt into which others sometimes fall. The written word was so clearly to him the voice of God, that anything that even appeared to call it in question was quite unthinkable and impossible as an interpretation. But though he could not understand unbelief and was shocked by it, his heart was so big and his sympathies so wide that he could love and treat with utmost courtesy the most active opponent.

Once when a friend spoke to him of some of the things maintained regarding Hinduism in its relation to Christianity by Madame Blavatsky and Mrs. Anne Besant, he said: "Alas! Alas! if they but knew real Hinduism; but, still more, if they but knew Christ, they could not think and say such things."

He lived to see a new nationalism in his country. The victory of Japan over Russia profoundly impressed every enlightened Asiatic. He felt that at last the tide of European aggression had been turned back, and that now the time had arrived for him to take a share in the movements of the nations. Dr. Chatterjee was himself an intense patriot, and welcomed the conservative Nationalism of the later years of his life. He felt that in the spread of this spirit was the great hope of India's advancement. But none could have deplored more than he the excesses into which many of his countrymen were led, or the assumption that England was in any sense the cause of the backward condition of the country. On the contrary, he recognized the fact that it was to England that India owed her emergence from the confusion, misrule, strife and degradation of the years preceding her acquisition of authority in the land. And more than this, he appreciated to the full, not only the invaluable services rendered in the past, but also shared in the fullest recognition on the part of India's people that her welfare for long years to come is inseparably connected with the maintenance of British authority in the country.

The subject of this sketch was as we have seen one of the leaders of the Christian Church in his country, gladly and cordially recognized as such by his brethren. Now that he has gone from us, may we not see in his life a message, left behind him, for the Church? If there be a message and there surely is one, it ought not to pass unrecognized and unheeded. From young manhood to old age, his life exemplified the motto, "This one thing I do." For himself he sought nothing in the way of material good and God wonderfully supplied all his need. Honors he looked not for, and was surprised when they came. Position he might have had; but by deliberate choice turned away from it for the sake of the Gospel. His was a happy and marvelously useful life. It ended with the words: "I am a servant of Jesus Christ." Beloved by all who knew him, honored by all who knew of him and his personality and work, his memory will abide in the Indian Church, a stimulus, we trust, to succeeding generations of young men, some of whom are even now asking, with real earnestness, where and in what spirit God would have them devote their lives.